MASTER

★ OF HIS ★

FATE

JAMES TOBIN

MASTER

★ OF HIS ★

FATE

ROOSEVELT'S RISE
FROM **POLIO** TO THE
PRESIDENCY

Christy Ottaviano Books

HENRY HOLT AND COMPANY

NEW YORK

Henry Holt and Company, *Publishers since 1866*
Henry Holt® is a registered trademark of Macmillan
Publishing Group, LLC
120 Broadway, New York, NY 10271 • mackids.com

Our books may be purchased for business or promotional
use. For information on bulk purchases, please contact your
local bookseller or the Macmillan Corporate and Premium
Sales Department at (800) 221-7945 x5442 or by email at
specialmarkets@macmillan.com.

Library of Congress Cataloging-in-Publication Data

Names: Tobin, James, 1956– author.
Title: Master of his fate : Roosevelt's rise from polio to the
presidency / James Tobin.
Other titles: Roosevelt's rise from polio to the presidency
Description: First edition. | New York : Christy Ottaviano
   Books, Henry Holt and Company, 2021. | Includes
   bibliographical references. | Audience: Ages 9–14 |
   Audience: Grades 4–6 | Summary: "A biography of FDR,
   focusing on his battle with polio and how his disease set
   him on the course to become president, for fans of Steve
   Sheinkin's political biographies"— Provided by publisher.
Identifiers: LCCN 2020020580 | ISBN 9781627795203
   (hardcover)
Subjects: LCSH: Roosevelt, Franklin D. (Franklin Delano),
   1882–1945—Juvenile literature. | Roosevelt, Franklin D.
   (Franklin Delano), 1882–1945—Health—Juvenile literature. |
   Presidents—United States—Biography—Juvenile
   literature. | Poliomyelitis—Patients—United States—
   Biography—Juvenile literature. | Presidents—United
   States—Election—1932—Juvenile literature.
Classification: LCC E807 .T635 2021 | DDC 973.917092 [B] —dc23
LC record available at https://lccn.loc.gov/2020020580

First Edition, 2021

Book design by Kay Petronio

Printed in the United States of America by
LSC Communications, Harrisonburg, Virginia

10 9 8 7 6 5 4 3 2 1

TO BEN
AND
LUCY

★ ★ ★

REMEMBER THIS
STORY WHEN
SOMEONE SAYS,
"YOU'LL NEVER BE ABLE
TO DO THAT."

CONTENTS

PREFACE

One day while Franklin Delano Roosevelt was president, someone asked him to name his favorite poem. His taste in reading ran more to factual matters, especially political history and geography—even atlases, which he studied so closely that he knew the elevations of various mountains around the world. But he did like one poem in particular, he said. The title was "Invictus." The author was an Englishman named William Ernest Henley (1849–1903).

It's a short poem that tells of the writer's determination to stay strong in the midst of terrible troubles. The title is Latin for "unconquerable."

> Out of the night that covers me,
> Black as the pit from pole to pole,
> I thank whatever gods may be
> For my unconquerable soul.
>
> In the fell clutch of circumstance
> I have not winced nor cried aloud.
> Under the bludgeonings of chance
> My head is bloody, but unbowed...
>
> It matters not how strait the gate,
> How charged with punishments the scroll,
> I am the master of my fate:
> I am the captain of my soul.

Why that poem?

Roosevelt may have known that William Ernest Henley suffered from Pott's disease, a painful form of tuberculosis that invades the bones. When Henley was sixteen, his left leg had to be amputated. At twenty-eight he was told he would lose his right leg, too. But he found a new surgeon who managed to save the leg in a series of delicate operations. In the hospital's recovery ward, Henley wrote "Invictus."

This book is about why "Invictus" spoke to and for Franklin Roosevelt.

At first, fate had been kind to him, placing him in a famous and wealthy family blessed with every advantage. But in 1921, when he was thirty-nine years old, fate turned cruel, cutting short the pursuit of his dreams.

That's where this story begins—with the "bludgeonings of chance" that suddenly fell upon Roosevelt. Then it tells about the decision he had to make—whether to drop back into a quiet life of comfort or to fight on. His choice revealed much about his character. What he did for the next ten years revealed much more, and that is the rest of the story.

The book ends just as Roosevelt is about to embark on his twelve years in the presidency. He was inaugurated on March 4, 1933, the deepest point of the Great Depression. He served until his death twelve years later, on April 12, 1945, near the end of World War II.

Those were the most dangerous years the American people had endured since the Civil War of the 1860s. Without Roosevelt's leadership, the crises of economic depression and war might have turned into catastrophes. When historians are asked to rank the country's greatest presidents, four names always appear at the top of the list: George Washington, Thomas Jefferson, Abraham Lincoln, and Franklin Roosevelt—or FDR, as he so often signed documents and letters, in bold, slashing diagonals that captured the vaulting energy of his personality.

To understand America in those hard times, you have to know who Franklin Roosevelt really was. As the journalist Joseph Alsop, a distant cousin of Roosevelt's, later wrote: "One of the central problems facing anyone dealing with Franklin Roosevelt's personal history is just what made him the man he became." This story is one of the keys that unlocks that mystery.

He followed a twisting path to the mastery of his fate. He learned that to be unconquerable was not a matter of sheer willpower. It was more complicated than that. It required seeing and facing the truth. It meant failing and starting again, then failing again and trying something new. It depended on flexibility and perseverance, not brute strength. By the time he reached the White House, he had learned that while no one hopes for misfortune, it can lead to unexpected opportunities and rewards—even to greatness.

———— ◆ ————

Writing a biography is like opening an old box full of the jumbled pieces of a jigsaw puzzle and then discovering that many pieces are missing.

Biographers search for the fragments of a person's life that have survived the passage of time—things like old letters written in scratchy handwriting, articles clipped out of forgotten newspapers, grainy black-and-white photos. Then they try to fit the fragments together to form a picture that captures the essence of the person's life.

Pieces are always missing. Some biographers spend decades searching for them. But the puzzle can never be complete, even when the subject is someone like Franklin Roosevelt, who kept just about everything and who was observed as closely and remembered as vividly as any American of the twentieth century. In his case, it sometimes seems as if the holes outnumber the pieces.

So . . . what to do?

We study the pieces that surround a hole and say to ourselves, *I bet I know what goes in that hole—it's obvious from the pieces all around it.*

Or we ask questions and suggest possible answers: *What goes there?*

Maybe this; maybe that. But we never know for sure which answer, if any, is right.

Some biographers pretend they've found every missing piece. They tell the story as if they know more than they really do.

Others are honest about the missing pieces. When they have questions they can't answer, they say so. They tell the reader when they're speculating.

Doing it the first way can make a story more readable. When all the missing parts are filled in, the biography reads more like a novel.

But if readers get suspicious—if they think, *Wait . . . does the author know that for sure?*—then the ground starts to shake beneath their feet. The readers don't know what to trust. They want a good story, yes, but when they read a biography, they also want the truth.

So I like doing it the second way—being straight with the reader about what's known for sure and what's educated guesswork. It's better to say, *I don't have every piece of the puzzle. I'll tell you when I'm speculating and when I have questions I can't answer for sure. I'll give you my best judgments. But that's what they are—not the absolute truth.*

Anyway, to me, the mystery of the missing pieces makes the past all the more fascinating.

Some people may object to the very idea of a biography of a privileged man who, as president, made certain decisions that now look wrongheaded, even hurtful.

But a biography is not a monument to its subject. It's not a marble statue to revere as if it symbolizes an ideal human being. Granted, Franklin Roosevelt was hardly that. For all his strengths, even greatness, he had his flaws as anyone does. He could be selfish and petty. He had biases and blind spots. But if we ignore him and others because they made what we now call mistakes, we run the risk of blinding ourselves.

A good biography is much more like a museum than a memorial. The book invites us into the subject's world, where we can watch them respond to challenges. We can study the personality behind the deeds. We can see how the world shapes the individual and how the individual shapes the world in turn. In a biography, as in life, that's the way we learn how to shape our own worlds.

———— ♦ ————

Readers will see that I occasionally use the offensive words "cripple" and "crippled." In recent times, our society has learned how damaging those words are. They imply that people with disabilities are somehow less valuable than people without disabilities—or, even worse, that people with disabilities should be hidden away or shunned. Those ideas are profoundly mistaken. Yet they were so common in Roosevelt's lifetime that few people thought twice about using the words that symbolize the ideas. This was and still is a major challenge for any person with a disability—to overcome the biases that exist in other people's minds. That was certainly true for Franklin Roosevelt, who wanted not only to live a full life but to lead his nation. So I've occasionally used the words that represent the powerful forces of ignorance and prejudice that opposed his ambitions. If readers never see these words, they may never understand just what he was up against.

PART 1

THE INFECTION

······························

AUGUST–OCTOBER 1921

Chapter 1

CAMPOBELLO

· ·

Franklin Roosevelt loved to tell stories about his life. He would talk about his ancestors who'd fought in the American Revolution, the towns he'd visited, the people he'd met, the friends he'd made, the moments he remembered.

But he never said much about what happened to him on Campobello Island in the summer of 1921.

At the age of thirty-nine, he was one of the most promising young politicians in the country. Many people thought he might one day be president of the United States. But events at his family's summer home on Campobello put an end to any such talk.

He had always loved the island. As a boy he spent fall, winter, and spring on his family's estate on the Hudson River, a hundred miles north of New York City. But at the start of every summer, Campobello beckoned. He learned to sail there, steering his own boat among the rocky islets and drifting mists of Passamaquoddy Bay, the great arm of the Atlantic Ocean that divides the tip of Maine from the Canadian province of New Brunswick. As he grew into manhood he went back nearly every year. After he married, he brought his wife, Eleanor, and their growing brood of children to their summer house overlooking the bay.

But after 1921, he went back to Campobello only three times, and then for the briefest of stays.

Many years later, one of his sons, Franklin Roosevelt Jr., was asked why his father had all but abandoned his favorite spot on earth. He replied: "I think he just couldn't bear to go back to the place where he had hiked and run and ridden horseback and climbed cliffs, and realize that he could never do those things again."

———————— ◆ ————————

The first hint that something was wrong came into his mind on an ocean-going yacht sailing up the coast of New England as the calendar turned from July to August.

FDR was heading for his first real vacation in a long time. Through the four years of World War I (1914–1918) and its aftermath, he had worked long, difficult hours as assistant secretary of the U.S. Navy under President Woodrow Wilson. In 1920, he had sprinted through a national political campaign as the Democratic Party's nominee for vice president. When that campaign failed, he had launched himself into a dozen new activities. Now, finally, he could look forward to two glorious weeks of recreation and rest.

He was aboard the yacht of his friend Van Lear Black, a millionaire businessman and sportsman from Baltimore. FDR had invited Black to bring his family and some friends up to Campobello for a few days. The Blacks picked him up in New York City; then they all sailed north together.

He had a wonderful time aboard. He would remind Black later that he "never laughed as much as we all did on the cruise up the Coast of Maine."

But he also felt a little sluggish and sick, as if he had picked up an intestinal bug.

Then he noticed something stranger. His skin was becoming unusually sensitive; his nerves seemed to be on high alert.

After two days on the water FDR spied Campobello on the horizon—a line of dark conifer trees on a craggy shore. He himself likely piloted the yacht through the tricky, narrow channel that divided the island from the village of Lubec at the easternmost tip of Maine. Campobello, though so close to the American mainland, belonged to Canada. Even in summer, not many people lived there—just a handful of Canadian fishermen, their families, and a scattering of Americans who loved the place for its crisp sea air and long views of the bay.

Roosevelt's parents—James and Sara Delano Roosevelt—had purchased property there in the 1880s because they thought it would be a healthy summer spot for their only child, who seemed to get sick so often. They had a fine house built, and twenty years later, when FDR married, his mother purchased an even finer house next door and gave it to the bride and groom. It was a broad, comfortable place with a red roof, loads of bedrooms, and wide windows overlooking the water.

A loud houseful of people greeted FDR and the Blacks. There was Eleanor Roosevelt, who was not only FDR's wife but his distant cousin, the favorite niece of the former president Theodore Roosevelt; FDR and Eleanor's daughter, Anna, who was fifteen; their four sons, James, thirteen; Elliott, ten; Franklin Jr., about to turn seven; and John, five; the children's nanny; the nanny's mother; and the family of Louis Howe, FDR's close friend and assistant.

For Roosevelt, free time meant time on the move outdoors. He was a sailor, golfer, and tennis player. In Washington, D.C., during the war, he had joined other government executives for daily workouts with a famous football coach. At work he often jogged from one appointment to the next. He took stairs two at a time.

So once he reached Campobello, he wasted no time lounging around. He announced the first order of business: a fishing expedition on Passamaquoddy Bay. The next morning, he and the others boarded Black's yacht and cruised out across the gray water. Then they got into the vessel's "tender" boat, a long, narrow craft with two cockpits, one at either end, with the engine taking up most of the space in between.

FDR gave himself the job of baiting fish hooks for everyone. To carry the hooks from one cockpit to the other, he had to step carefully along a narrow, wet plank beside the hot engine.

Suddenly he lost his footing and plunged into the water. It took only a minute for the others to haul him back on board, and right away he was laughing at himself.

"All you landlubbers" were still dry on board, he said, yet he was the one, an "old salt" with many years on the water, who had become the only "man overboard."

Funny thing, that slip. He'd been dashing around slippery boat decks forever. He'd hardly ever fallen off a boat. Yet that day he had done it. And although he had been swimming in the frigid water there for many years, it never had felt as cold as it did that day—"so cold," he remembered later, "it seemed paralyzing."

———————◆———————

Once the Blacks had gone, FDR turned to having fun with his children. "Father loved life on the island more than any of us, but got to spend the least time there," remembered Jimmy, the oldest boy. In this family, fun was strenuous. They played tennis. They went swimming and sailing. They played a pursuit game FDR loved called Hare and Hounds, which sent the players racing up and down the rocky slopes along the shore. For two or three days, Jimmy remembered, they had "a wild, whooping, romping, running, sailing, picnicking time."

On the morning of Wednesday, August 10, FDR arose from his bed feeling worn out, though he had slept all night. He thought another good day outdoors might restore his energy. So he piled everyone into the family's sailboat, *Vireo*, and steered for a deserted island out in the bay. On the beach they shared a picnic lunch. Then, sailing for home, they spotted smoke rising from an island in the distance—a forest fire.

At his home in upstate New York, FDR raised trees as a hobby. He couldn't bear to see trees destroyed. So he steered toward the smoke and beached the boat. The family tumbled out to fight the fire. Other people who had spotted the smoke joined them. For hours, the Roosevelts worked as an emergency fire brigade, swatting at flames with evergreen branches and stamping on sparks. Anna was standing near a tall spruce when she heard "that awful roar of the flames as they quickly enveloped the whole tree." They sweated in the heat and smoke until the fire was finally out.

After an outing like that, most families would have been ready to collapse on the couch. But when the Roosevelts got back to the cottage, someone suggested a swim. FDR was still feeling that unfamiliar sluggishness. He thought a quick dip might drive the feeling away. So he and the children set off at a jogging pace for Lake Glensevern, a long, narrow pond with water warm enough for comfortable swimming. It was about a mile and a half away. They all dove in. While the children splashed around, FDR left the pond and ran a little farther for a plunge in the colder waters of the ocean. Then they all straggled back along the trail toward home and dinner.

In the living room, FDR dropped into a wicker chair. He said he was too tired even to change into dry clothes. He just wanted to sit still. "I'd never felt quite that way before," he remarked later. He and his friend Louis Howe paged through the newspapers and opened mail.

After a while Eleanor called everyone to dinner.

"About halfway through the meal," their daughter, Anna, remembered later, "Father very quietly announced that he thought he had a slight attack of lumbago"—pain in the lower back. He felt a chill, too, he said, and he wanted to get completely warm. "He thought he'd better excuse himself and go up to bed. There was no fuss."

He rose, walked across the room, and climbed the stairs.

———— ◆ ————

When he awoke the next morning, his legs hurt. He swung them out of bed, placed his feet on the floor, and stood up.

There was something wrong with his knee, the right one. He must have twisted it the day before without noticing, maybe while fighting the forest fire. Or maybe he had slept on it wrong.

From the bedroom, he crossed the hallway to the bathroom. He stood at the sink to shave. That knee—it felt as if it couldn't hold his weight. He went back to bed.

Eleanor sent Anna upstairs with breakfast on a tray. FDR could see his daughter was worried. He reassured her and they joked for a couple minutes.

But when Anna was back downstairs and Eleanor looked in, he told her he was feeling dreadful. He couldn't understand it, but his legs were killing him.

Elliott was standing nearby. Many years later, he remembered that his father used the words "stabbing pains." Others who have gone through the same experience say it felt like someone was hammering nails into their legs.

———— ◆ ————

Eleanor sent a message from the island over to the mainland village of Lubec. She wanted the family's summertime doctor to see Franklin. His name was Eben Homer Bennet.

Dr. Bennet got to the island that afternoon. He asked questions and took FDR's temperature. It was 102 degrees, quite high but not dangerous. He concluded the problem was a severe summer cold. He couldn't explain why Roosevelt's legs were bothering him.

In the afternoon, FDR went to stand up, then abruptly sat back down. Now his right knee definitely could not support his weight. By evening, the other knee was feeling weak.

By the next morning, August 12, the needles of pain had spread to his back. He couldn't clench the muscles of his buttocks or his gut. It wasn't that his muscles were numb. If he rubbed his legs with his hands, he could feel his hands. But the muscles wouldn't obey his commands to move.

His arms felt weak. That evening he reached for a pencil. His fingers couldn't hold it.

The fever rose so high that he drifted in and out of delirium.

By now his legs felt like the floppy legs of a marionette. He couldn't walk. He couldn't stand up.

He stared at Howe.

"I don't know what is the matter with me, Louis," he said. "I just don't know."

———— ◆ ————

By the next day, Eleanor and Howe realized the problem must be something much worse than a summer cold. They had to find another doctor, one with more experience than their friend Dr. Bennet.

There wasn't a telephone on all of the island. So Howe had a boat take him over the channel to Lubec. There he made long-distance calls to resorts in southern Maine, where he hoped to find some prominent doctor on summer vacation. In the wealthy resort town of Bar Harbor, far down the coast, he located a famous surgeon named William Williams Keen.

Dr. Keen wasn't the perfect choice. He'd been retired for nearly fifteen years. He was eighty-four years old. But he had treated other famous patients, including former president Grover Cleveland. He was still respected. And he wasn't too far away.

So Howe asked: Would Dr. Keen make the trip up to Campobello to examine Franklin Roosevelt?

He said he would.

Keen was indeed a prominent doctor, but he was a surgeon. Surgeons cut people open to fix or remove damaged or diseased body parts—organs, bones, arteries, muscles. Since his earliest days as a doctor on the battlefields of the Civil War, Keen had been cutting, repairing, and stitching. He was not accustomed to diagnosing the causes of mysterious pain and paralysis.

He got to the island late in the day on Saturday, August 13.

A small man with a neat beard, the old surgeon leaned over his tall young patient, asking questions, tapping for reflexes, prodding muscles. He pondered. The next morning, he did the exam all over again.

At last he gave his diagnosis. Mr. Roosevelt had a blood clot in his lower spine, he said. It was pressing on nerves that controlled his leg muscles. That was causing the paralysis.

The clot, he said, probably had formed when FDR took that sudden plunge in icy water when he was fishing. Overexertion in the days since had made it worse.

The paralysis of his legs would pass as the clot slowly dissolved, the doctor said, though it might take quite a long time.

Massage his legs, Dr. Keen told Eleanor. *It will hurt, but it might get rid of that blood clot.*

Then he left the island.

Eleanor rubbed her husband's legs. The pain became all but unbearable.

———————◆———————

Hour after hour, Louis Howe watched his friend suffer.

Howe was a newspaperman who had dropped his old career to become a political jack-of-all-trades, helping politicians with speeches, correspondence, and organizing. He had spotted Roosevelt as a young up-and-comer in the New York state senate and had worked for him ever since. Their professional relationship had evolved into a close friendship—Howe like an older brother, more experienced and cynical; Roosevelt the younger brother, needing advice and a firm hand.

In his fifty years, Howe had spent a lot of time with doctors. Small and homely, as he was the first to admit, he had been sickly since childhood and prone to bad luck. As a boy he had taken a bad fall that left tiny specks of gravel permanently embedded in the skin of his face. As an adult he developed serious asthma and heart disease. Doctors warned him so often about his precarious health that he once told FDR, "Sooner or later I [will] ignore the danger signals too long and drop out like a snuffed candle."

He kept ignoring the signals because he didn't think doctors knew much, even famous ones like Dr. Keen.

As a reporter, Howe had learned to notice things that other people missed. Now he was noticing conditions in the house that Dr. Keen apparently had overlooked.

Several people in the Roosevelt household that week—including Howe's wife, Grace, and a couple of the children—had come down with fevers and chills of their own, though there was no problem in their limbs. The symptoms were not as bad as FDR's, but still, Howe reasoned, didn't it seem likely that if several people in the same house were sick, there was a common cause? And surely all these people didn't have blood clots in their spinal cords.

So it seemed to Howe the cause must be an infectious germ. If so, which one? What germ could cause symptoms like the flu in one person and paralysis in someone else?

Howe always kept close track of the news. Even at distant Campobello, the Roosevelts had the New York newspapers sent to them. Over the last couple of weeks, the papers had carried small reports of a dangerous disease, just a few cases here and there across upstate New York.

The disease had two names. Most people called it infantile paralysis, because it usually struck babies and small children, who suddenly lost strength in one or more of their limbs. The scientific name was poliomyelitis—or polio, for short.

Maybe Howe had seen the news reports. Maybe he hadn't. But something made him suspect that Dr. Keen was wrong about a clot in FDR's spine and that infantile paralysis might be the cause of the trouble.

Without telling Eleanor, Howe sent a telegram to FDR's uncle, Frederic Delano, who worked for the government in Washington. Delano knew many important people and was good at getting difficult things done.

Please, Howe said, *find an expert on poliomyelitis as quickly as possible.*

———————————•◆•———————————

In Washington, Fred Delano called his son-in-law, a doctor, who said Delano should consult the Harvard Infantile Paralysis Commission in Cambridge, Massachusetts. Uncle Fred was soon in touch with Dr. Robert Lovett, head of the commission. Lovett was an orthopedist—a bone doctor—and a professor at Harvard University. He agreed to make the long trip up to Campobello.

On August 24, two weeks after FDR had gone upstairs with pain in his lower back, Eleanor Roosevelt greeted Dr. Lovett, a quiet, handsome, serious man with a dark mustache turning gray. Upstairs, he examined FDR. Then he inserted a thick needle into Roosevelt's spine and drew some fluid out of the spinal cord. The procedure causes terrible pain. But it had to be done to confirm the diagnosis. In a healthy person, the spinal fluid is clear. If it looks cloudy, it's full of the white cells that fight infection—a clear sign of a virus in the spinal cord. Lovett had to be sure.

He looked at the fluid.

It was cloudy white.

Infection in the spinal cord combined with paralyzed limbs meant that Roosevelt had contracted poliomyelitis.

He gave the news to FDR and Eleanor.

Many years later, near the end of her life, someone asked Eleanor about that moment. How had her husband looked when he heard what Dr. Lovett said?

She thought about it, then remarked that she had seen a certain expression on FDR's face only twice in all the time she knew him.

Once was that moment with Dr. Lovett at Campobello.

The other was twenty years later, on December 7, 1941, when FDR was told that Japanese fighter planes had attacked U.S. ships at Pearl Harbor, Hawaii, drawing the United States into World War II.

"His reaction to any great event," she remembered another time, "was always to be calm. If it was something that was bad, he just became almost like an iceberg, and there was never the slightest emotion that was allowed to show . . . I have never known him not to be ready to face the worst that could happen, but always to be hopeful about the solution that could be found."

Chapter 2

QUESTIONS

•••••••••••••••••••••••••••

The Roosevelts struggled to make sense of what Dr. Lovett had told them.

What they knew about infantile paralysis consisted of little more than fading memories of a terrible epidemic five years earlier.

There had been isolated outbreaks in the United States starting in the 1890s. Then, in the summer of 1916, the disease made headlines with a far worse outbreak than any before. It was centered in New York City. Some nine thousand people were paralyzed, many of them babies. The Roosevelts were fearful their own children might catch the disease. Working in Washington, far away from the family, FDR wrote to Eleanor and urged her to swat every fly she saw, since flies were suspected of spreading the contagion.

There had been more cases in the years since, but nowhere near as many, and the polio panic of that wartime summer faded.

The news stories of 1916 had described terribly sick *children*, not adults.

Reporters focused on immigrant children in the dirty, close-packed city neighborhoods called slums—children dying or crippled, with twisted legs and arms; children rushed out of the city to escape the danger of infection. When the Roosevelts thought about infectious diseases, they pictured filthy streets and squalid houses with bad plumbing. Those were hardly the sort of surroundings in which *they* lived.

So how could FDR—a healthy, vigorous man of thirty-nine who lived and worked in fine buildings that were cleaned every day—get *that* disease?

Wasn't it possible, they asked, that something else explained FDR's condition, something less serious and frightening?

Dr. Lovett could only shrug and say that adults sometimes *did* catch the virus that caused infantile paralysis, even adults as healthy as FDR. The truth was shocking, but he had no doubt about it.

"I detected some uncertainty in their minds about the diagnosis," Dr. Lovett said later, "but I thought it perfectly clear."

The Roosevelts must have asked Lovett where the virus had come from. How had FDR contracted it? And how could this have happened when there was no widespread epidemic?

Dr. Lovett could answer only a few of their questions. Medical scientists were largely mystified about even the most basic facts. They knew the sickness was caused by an impossibly tiny germ called the poliovirus. But it would be many years before scientists detected how the virus spread; or why polio struck in summer; or why it appeared in one region but not another; or why it targeted the young. Doctors knew by 1921 that only a fraction of the people who caught the virus became paralyzed, perhaps one in a thousand. But they had no idea why one person recovered while another became paralyzed or even died.

As to the where and how of FDR's infection, Dr. Lovett may have asked, *Have you been around any children lately?*

Not his own children. They had been at Campobello.

But near the end of July, he had spent several hours with a large group of children—Boy Scouts, hundreds of them.

———— ◆ ————

It had been just another appointment on his calendar. Indeed, Roosevelt's calendar in 1921 was crammed with events like his visit to the Boy Scout campgrounds north of New York City on July 27. They made up the everyday rounds of a man who meant one day to run for president.

For most Americans, aiming for the White House would be a wild long shot, but not for Franklin Roosevelt.

To start with, he had the most famous name in American politics. He was related by both blood and marriage to Theodore Roosevelt, who had died just two years earlier after a thundering career as a crusading politician, cowboy, writer, war hero, and president.

And FDR had accomplishments of his own. He had been a state senator, then assistant secretary of the navy. In 1920 the Democrats chose him to run for vice president with Governor James Cox of Ohio, the presidential nominee. They lost that race, but FDR made a good showing across the country and proved that "another Roosevelt" was on the rise in politics.

Now, after eight years in Washington, he intended to reestablish himself as a public figure in his home state of New York. Soon he would run for statewide office, and then, when the time was right, he would run for president. In the meantime, he planned to do good things and make influential friends in as many civic and charitable organizations as possible. One of these groups was the Boy Scouts of Greater New York. He had agreed to become chairman of the organization because he thought highly of the Scouts—two of his sons were members—and because it was one more way to meet and befriend important New Yorkers who were volunteering their time to help the boys.

Every summer, Boy Scouts from New York City and its suburbs gathered for weeklong outings at campgrounds near the massive hump of Bear Mountain, fifty miles north of the city. On July 27 there was to be a giant cookout, so FDR and other supporters of the Scouts made a day trip out of it, cruising up the Hudson River to Bear Mountain, then jouncing over dirt roads by car to join hundreds of Scouts for an outdoor supper.

Somewhere at Bear Mountain, it seems clear, there was a virus too small to be seen with even the most powerful microscope available in 1921. If five thousand such viruses were placed in a single-file line, they would barely reach from one edge of a grain of salt to the other. That made it one of the smallest viruses ever discovered. Despite the havoc it could cause, as it had in 1916, the virus was very common and not very dangerous—not for most people, anyway. It was dangerous only if it found its way into a person with a particular vulnerability, and if, by pure chance, it slipped into the wrong part of that person's body.

In 1921 no one knew the poliovirus passed from one person to another via tiny specks of human waste. An infected bit of human feces could have reached the campground by any of a number of paths.

It might have turned up on the hand of one of the Boy Scouts. If so, it's not hard to imagine how it got there. The boy could have picked up the virus a few days earlier when he changed his baby brother's diaper. The virus could have entered the Scout's system without making him sick—again, most people who caught it never got sick at all—so his parents would have had no reason to keep him home from the campout. Then maybe the Scout used the outdoor toilet at the campground and forgot to wash his hands. Then he might have grabbed a piece of fried chicken from a platter on a picnic table—but right then maybe his friend called him away and he put the chicken back. And then maybe Franklin Roosevelt picked up the chicken leg and took a bite.

Or the virus may have been in a cup of drinking water. Just a few months earlier, the New York Department of Health had sent an expert to see if Bear Mountain's lakes and streams were safe for swimming and drinking. The expert tested the water and said, no, the water definitely was *not* safe. There weren't enough toilets for the large number of people visiting the state parks in the area. The expert found signs of human feces in the lakes and streams. So the poliovirus might have been in the water, too. But the state didn't close the parks. If the Boy Scouts pumped water from wells fed by underground streams or dipped water from the lake, the virus might have been in the water they drank at the cookout, and it could have ended up in a cup of water served to FDR.

Or maybe the boy who forgot to wash his hands ran straight up to the famous man who was the cousin of the great Teddy Roosevelt and stuck out his hand to shake. FDR was a politician, and a good politician shakes every hand that comes along.

Later, scientists would discover that it takes ten to fourteen days for the poliovirus to cause noticeable symptoms. The day of the forest fire, when he felt the first pains in his lower back and went to bed early, was August 10, fourteen days after his trip to Bear Mountain.

———•◆•———

The food or fluid in FDR's mouth carried the virus into his throat, where it may have lodged in the tonsils. Or it may have gone down the throat and entered the twenty-foot-long coiled tube called the small intestine, which has a velvety lining that absorbs water and nutrients. The cells of that lining have microscopic branches. One virus, maybe many, bumped into those branches and stuck like a ball lodged in a tree.

A strange process began. The virus didn't just hang on the branch of that unlucky cell. It connected with the branch like a key in a lock, then released its own genes into the cell. Inside, the virus commandeered the cell's tiny machinery, and then, as if in a sorcerer's factory, it began to churn out copies of itself—first by the dozens, then by the thousands, too many for the cell to contain. The cell exploded, sending new viral pioneers through the bloodstream.

Hour after hour, the process repeated itself. New viruses invaded new cells and cranked out more copies. One after another, the cells burst, sending more viruses downstream to find more cells to destroy.

The multiplying virus triggered a reaction from FDR's immune system, the vast network of cells whose job was to swarm around viruses and bacteria and kill them.

But it seems that FDR's immune system had never been very strong.

At his parents' country estate at Hyde Park, New York, one hundred miles north of New York City, he had grown up as an only child, and his mother seldom allowed him to play with the few children who lived nearby. He didn't go to school for the early grades. He was taught at home by private tutors. So he never caught many of the germs that most children pass around and develop a resistance to in their early years.

In high school and college he came down with scarlet fever, measles, mumps, and dozens of sinus infections and colds. On his honeymoon in 1905, he had hives—itchy lumps on the skin that can be caused by a sputtering immune system. While he was assistant secretary of the navy, he had appendicitis, two severe throat infections, influenza, double pneumonia, and tonsillitis. His boss at the navy department said FDR seemed to catch every bug that came along.

In most people who caught the poliovirus, immune cells would kill it and send it out of the body in the urine and feces before it could cause any trouble. In one person out of ten, there would be symptoms like the ones caused by an ordinary "flu bug"—fever and chills, a stomachache, a headache, sluggishness. But the immune system would win out, the symptoms would vanish, and the incident would be forgotten.

In Roosevelt's case, the virus went up a wrong alley and passed through a filtering system that doctors call the blood-brain barrier. Normally, that barrier keeps harmful particles in the bloodstream out of the nervous system. But the poliovirus is small enough to pass through the filter. When it does, it turns dangerous.

The nervous system is a fabulously complex network of cables that carry electrical signals between the brain and the rest of the body. One set of cables transmits sensations—hot or cold, rough or smooth, wet or dry, painful or pleasant. A second set of cables controls the movements of the muscles. The signals move at unimaginable speeds through long, threadlike nerve cells called neurons. The cables are built in sections, each section linked to the next, strung by the billions through all parts of the body. The number of cellular cables in the body is flabbergasting—about one hundred billion. If the nerve cables in a single human body were laid out end to end, they would stretch for ninety thousand miles.

In the spinal cord, neurons come to junctions called horn cells. (The cells live in a part of the cord that looks a bit like the horn of a trumpet.) Some are in the front—the *anterior* horn cells. Some are in the back—the *posterior* horn cells. The posterior cells carry the signals of the senses—seeing, hearing, smelling, touching. The anterior cells carry the signals that tell the muscles what to do.

The poliovirus only locks with the *anterior* horn cells, the ones controlling muscle movement. No one knows why the virus works that way, but when it happens, just as in the intestines, the virus penetrates a nerve cell and cranks out so many copies of itself that the cell explodes and dies. Then the process repeats itself over and over, wiping out more and more anterior horn cells.

Imagine the brain sending a signal to the big toe of a healthy person's right foot, telling the toe to wiggle. The signal flashes down the spinal cord to an anterior horn cell, which routes the signal smoothly down to the toe— and the toe moves.

But if the poliovirus has destroyed that horn cell, the brain's electrical signal just stops. The toe never gets the signal. Nothing's wrong with the muscles and bones in the toe. They *can* work. They just don't.

A nerve cell that dies can never come back to life. But that's not a problem as long as a person doesn't lose too many. The body has many more nerve cells than it needs, including anterior horn cells. So other cells pick up the slack. They carry the brain's signal to the toe, just by a different series of cables.

But if too many cells die, the signal begins to stutter, and little things start to go wrong—hypersensitivity in the sensory nerves, for example, and weakness in the limbs.

There were no news reports that Boy Scouts who attended the Bear Mountain campout had come down with infantile paralysis.

So why only FDR?

Here, too, Dr. Lovett could not have said much. It might have been just a million-to-one case of bad luck. But there were two reasons why FDR may have been particularly susceptible to the poliovirus.

First, he simply may have been born with a weak immune system. His tendency from an early age to pick up infections suggests this was so.

Then there was the physical environment of his childhood, which may have made his immune system even weaker.

When we hear about infectious diseases, we think of bad sanitation. We think of places with polluted water and no toilets and people who haven't washed their hands.

The strange truth about polio is that it tends to spread where sanitation is good.

In the 1880s, when FDR was a boy, almost nobody had a flush toilet, and few cities and towns had sewer systems to pipe human waste away for decontamination. So people's waste was stored in underground pits, and the stuff sometimes spread through the ground to wells where drinking water was drawn. In many places people relieved themselves in chamber pots, also called slop jars and thunder mugs, and then emptied the pots into the streets. (The smell was horrific. People approaching a big city like New York in the mid-1800s could smell it from miles away.)

One way or another, even if people tried hard to keep their homes clean, human feces spread through water and dirt and dust. That meant the poliovirus spread, too. It got into pretty much everybody, including babies.

That sounds dangerous, but it seldom was. Babies have extra-powerful immune cells passed to them from their mothers. In practically every baby, those cells would overwhelm the poliovirus. At the same time, the baby's own immune system would create special polio-fighting cells called lymphocytes. They stay in the body forever, so if the poliovirus reenters that person later in life, those anti-polio lymphocytes stop the virus cold.

All this means that in the 1800s, just about everyone grew up with a natural immunity to polio. That's why so few people came down with the disease.

Until the coming of toilets and sewers.

By the late 1800s, people in the fast-growing cities of North America got so fed up with the smell and the danger of so much human waste that they started building good sewer systems and installing flush toilets. Not everywhere, but in a lot of places.

When that happened, things changed for the poliovirus, too. There weren't so many specks of human waste passed from hand to hand. In places with good plumbing and sewers and plenty of clean water, children began to grow up without ever catching the poliovirus. So they never developed those special polio-fighting immune cells. As the years went by, more towns and cities were full of children without that immunity.

Good sanitation systems didn't kill the poliovirus. They just kept it out of the neighborhood. So if someone carrying the virus visited one of those places with good sanitation, the virus could cause a lot of trouble.

Sure enough, in the 1890s and 1900s, polio epidemics followed in the footsteps of the sanitation revolution in places like Boston, Massachusetts, and Rutland, Vermont, where the sanitation systems were good.

But nobody made the connection between polio and good sewers—not yet. In the great polio epidemic of 1916, people feared that polio was spreading in dirty, crowded neighborhoods where poor people lived. It was only later, when experts took a closer look, that they noticed polio was more likely to strike in middle- and upper-class neighborhoods, where sanitation was better. They didn't know why.

What did all this have to do with Franklin Roosevelt?

He had been raised on a country estate with plenty of clean water drawn from a spring behind his house. He had no brothers or sisters, only a much older half-brother. He seldom played with other kids. So it's likely that the young Franklin Roosevelt never came within a country mile of the poliovirus. And because he probably never picked up and fought off the poliovirus as a child, he lacked the disease-fighting lymphocytes that might have protected him when bad luck struck years later at Bear Mountain.

There might have been one more factor to blame.

Once the poliovirus gets into the nervous system, there's no telling how many cells it will destroy, or which parts of the body will be affected, before the immune cells kill it off.

In some people, the virus creeps on and on, climbing up the spinal cord until it reaches the brain. In the worst cases, the nerves that control the automatic in-and-out process of breathing can be ravaged. In those cases, many victims die. In other people, the attack on the nervous system promptly stalls right after it starts, leaving hardly any damage at all.

Doctors have never discovered why one attack is deadly, another mild. But they're sure about one thing: In a case that might go either way, mild or severe, the best thing the infected person can do is go to bed and rest. The immune cells need as much of the body's energy as they can get. The worst thing to do is to get a lot of hard exercise, the sort of exercise that comes with several days of "whooping, romping, [and] running" with young children and then spending an afternoon fighting a forest fire.

———————•◆•———————

The Roosevelts must have asked Dr. Lovett: *What about the future?* When would FDR be able to stand up and walk again? Was there any danger that his legs would be permanently paralyzed?

Dr. Lovett chose his words carefully.

Roosevelt was famous and powerful. Even a doctor as experienced as Dr. Lovett would hesitate to tell such a person that he may face a future radically different from his past.

Dr. Lovett knew perfectly well that at this early stage of the disease, no doctor could predict exactly what would happen. It all depended on how many nerve cells had been wiped out. And on the surplus nerves that might or might not take up the slack. And on the patient himself—would he be tough enough to fight for a strong recovery?

But it's difficult for a doctor to tell everything he knows to a patient who has just been given a shocking diagnosis. It may even hurt the patient. A good doctor knows that for many patients, the chance of recovery depends partly on the state of the patient's mind. If the patient loses hope, the body seems to lose hope, too. But if a patient is optimistic and determined, sometimes the body follows the mind's lead.

So Dr. Lovett spoke truthfully. But he also gave the Roosevelts reason to hope.

Compared to the worst cases he'd seen, this one was fairly mild, even "within the range of possible complete recovery," he said.

A few days later, Dr. Lovett described his talk with the Roosevelts in a letter to their personal doctor in New York. Lovett wrote: "I told them very frankly that no one could tell where they stood, that the case was evidently not of the severest type, that complete or partial recovery to any point was possible."

He also told the Roosevelts that "disability was not to be feared."

Now, Dr. Lovett was well aware that *some* degree of disability was quite possible. So he must have meant only that *complete* disability was not to be feared. That is, FDR would not have to stay flat on his back for the rest of his life. Eventually he'd be able to get up and move around, though probably with metal braces on his legs and crutches.

Eleanor was anxious about her children. Were they in danger?

Almost surely not, Lovett said. The flu-like symptoms that Louis Howe had noticed in the children after FDR's arrival might have been caused by the poliovirus. But if so, the children's immune systems had fought it off. And now their father was no longer contagious.

Dr. Lovett said FDR would have to rest at Campobello for several weeks before going home to New York. In the meantime, Eleanor should stop the painful massage. It was doing no good. In fact, it might be damaging FDR's muscles. After a few weeks they would see where things stood, then decide what to do next.

Dr. Lovett said he was very sorry, but the only thing to do was to wait and see what would happen. The worst would soon be over. At that point FDR could expect to feel some strength returning in the damaged muscles.

The doctor got ready to leave. Louis Howe asked him for a private word.

Howe wanted a straight answer to the hardest question: What were the chances that FDR would walk again?

Lovett decided to level with Howe.

It was just barely possible, he said. It would take "the most extraordinary will and patience" over a long period of time—"hours, days, weeks, months and years of constant effort."

And even if FDR worked that hard for that long, Lovett said, no one could guarantee he would ever again walk on his own.

Chapter 3

"HARD, CRUEL FACTS"

Day after day FDR lay in his bed, waiting.

He listened as Howe read aloud from the newspapers. When Eleanor came in to wash him or to help him relieve himself in a bedpan, all he could do was push his body up a bit from the bed with his hands and arms. Again and again he tried to move his legs. Nothing.

Another man who had polio described what this felt like. "You drive the thought of it with all your might down from your mind toward the lifeless leg," he wrote. "But the thought doesn't get there. Some deadly barrier lies between."

It was like what happens when you sleep half the night with your arm pinned under you. When you wake up, the arm feels heavy and dead, as if a big bag of sand has been tied to your body.

The quiet days passed. Eleanor let the children come to the door of FDR's bedroom to say hello and chat for a minute.

"He grinned at us," Jimmy Roosevelt remembered, "and he did his best to call out, or gasp out, some cheery response to our tremulous, just-this-side-of-tears greetings."

Eleanor and Louis broke the news to a few close relatives and friends in careful letters. Howe sent a brief notice to the newspapers saying only that FDR had been "seriously ill" but was "now improving."

Howe was keeping back the whole truth partly because FDR's mother, Sara Roosevelt, was about to set sail for the United States after a summer in Europe. They didn't want Sara to be shocked by a newspaper story saying FDR had infantile paralysis.

When making any family decision, Franklin and Eleanor had to think carefully about his mother.

Since the death of her husband, James Roosevelt, when Franklin was in college, Sara had been a wealthy woman. She had inherited her husband's substantial fortune and the estate on the Hudson River. This was the place FDR considered his true home, and the whole family—Sara, Franklin, Eleanor, and the children—spent many weekends and holidays there together. But Franklin's work as a politician and lawyer required a base in New York City, too. So their main address was 49 East Sixty-Fifth Street in Manhattan, a fine, six-story townhouse. Sara had given that house to the couple as a wedding gift and then moved in next door at No. 47, with doors connecting the twin houses on alternate floors.

The bonds between Sara and "my children," as she called Franklin and Eleanor, were strong but often strained. Sara covered many of the family's expenses, which gave her a silent source of power in many family decisions. And she worried about the welfare of her only child as if he were still a boy in school. If Franklin—a grown man with five children of his own—said he was about to leave the house on a rainy day, Sara would warn him that he *must* wear his rubber boots.

So they had to think carefully about how Sara would learn that her son was half-paralyzed, and they certainly didn't want her to read about it in the newspapers.

They had to tell other friends and associates, too, though how much they said depended on the person.

To FDR's secretary, a highly capable young woman named Marguerite LeHand, Eleanor wrote only that her husband had caught "a severe chill . . . which resulted in fever & much congestion."

FDR's own first letter from Campobello went to Langdon Marvin, his friend and partner in the New York law firm of Emmet, Marvin & Roosevelt. He had to let the firm know he would not be able to work for some time. He was more honest than Eleanor had been with Miss LeHand, though he tried hard to sound upbeat.

"My case has been diagnosed by Dr. Lovett as one of poliomyelitis," he wrote, "otherwise [known as] infantile paralysis. Cheerful thing for one with my gray hairs to get. I am almost wholly out of commission as to my legs but the doctors say that there is no question that I will get their use back again though this means several months of treatment in New York."

————— ◆ —————

He was not getting better.

Day after day, the muscles of his legs and buttocks were shriveling. At first he could barely notice the change, but soon it became obvious.

Muscles have to move to stay healthy. Otherwise their cells start to die, and the muscles wither. It seemed impossible, but FDR's legs were getting skinnier by the day.

Above the waist, he was feeling a bit better. The hint of paralysis in his hands had disappeared. His arms felt stronger. But his legs . . .

Dr. Bennet was dropping in often to see FDR. Finally he sent a telegram to Dr. Lovett, who was now back in Boston.

FDR was feeling "much anxiety," Bennet wrote. "Can you recommend anything to keep up his courage?"

No, Dr. Lovett wrote back, he had nothing more to say. There was nothing to do but wait and see how many muscles would recover on their own.

———— ◆ ————

On the first day of September, a week after Dr. Lovett left Campobello, Sara Roosevelt arrived on the island. She had stepped off the ship in New York to find her brother Fred waiting for her. He gave her the news. Now, with Eleanor and Dr. Bennet, she hurried up the stairs to her only child's sickbed.

FDR, still on his back, beamed his old smile.

"Well, I'm glad you are back, Mummy, and I got up this party for you!"

Sara "controlled herself remarkably," Eleanor recalled.

FDR chattered away, asking questions about her summer trip.

Dr. Bennet was all smiles, too, saying: "This boy is going to get well!"

That night Sara sat in a room by herself, writing letters to her sisters and brothers.

"I hear them all laughing, Eleanor in the lead," she wrote. "He and Eleanor decided at once to be cheerful and the atmosphere of the house is all happiness. So I have fallen in and follow their glorious example . . .

"Below his waist he cannot move at all. His legs (that I have always been so proud of) have to be moved often as they ache when long in one position . . . They have *no* power . . . He looks well and eats well and is very keen and full of interest in everything . . . Dr. Lovett, the greatest authority we have on infantile paralysis . . . says he *will* get well."

———— ◆ ————

FDR may have fooled his mother into thinking he was feeling "very keen." But we can be sure that underneath his show of good cheer, he was struggling against panic.

Anyone who suddenly can't walk is going to feel shocked and frightened. A "state of nervous collapse" is typical at first, according to one polio expert. All your life you take it for granted that your body will do what you tell it to do. Then one day it refuses to obey.

In a situation like this, people tend to follow the examples set by their families. That's what FDR was doing when he tried so hard to be cheerful. He had been taught not to "whine about trouble," and so had Eleanor.

Both of them knew about Theodore Roosevelt's ordeals in his youth—how he had fought the smothering effects of severe asthma by building himself up with tireless exercise; and how, when his young wife, Alice, had died, he had thrown himself into strenuous adventures on horseback. "Black care rarely sits behind a rider whose pace is fast enough," Theodore once wrote, "at any rate, not when he first feels the horse move under him." FDR certainly couldn't ride a horse, not right now, but his instincts were telling him to follow the spirit of Theodore's advice—to fight his anxiety and sadness with action.

From the Delano side of his family—his mother's side—he got advice along the same line.

Franklin's uncle, Fred Delano, the one who had persuaded Dr. Lovett to visit Campobello, had been wondering what else he might do to help. He sat down to write Franklin "some 'fatherly' advice."

Franklin must keep a cool head, Delano said. He must analyze his new problem as he would any other. He must not fool himself into thinking things were better than they really were. Doctors could help, but "the construction work of getting well depends largely on your own character . . .

"I realize you are up against a hard problem, and hard, cruel facts . . . I feel so confident of your background of health and good habits, and of your courage and good temper, that I refuse to be cast down."

———— ◆ ————

By the middle of September, more than a month after the earliest symptoms, the doctors said FDR was ready to travel by train to New York, where he would stay in Presbyterian Hospital, not far from the Roosevelts' townhouse, for several more weeks of rest.

The older children, Anna and Jimmy and Elliott, had already left Campobello to return to their boarding schools. Eleanor was to go with Franklin on the train. The younger boys, Franklin Jr., seven, and John, five, would stay on the island a bit longer with their governess while their parents got settled at home.

Eleanor had told Franklin and John simply that their father was very ill and couldn't play with them for a while. She didn't try to explain what polio was.

They had hardly seen him for weeks. They heard the adults talking but couldn't really tell what was wrong.

Franklin Jr. thought he heard one of his older brothers say something about a heart attack, which he knew was very serious.

John Roosevelt watched four men carry his father down the stairs on a stretcher, then cross the lawn to the bay, where a boat was waiting to take him to the train station at Eastport, Maine.

"He managed to wave to me," John remembered many years later, "and his whole face burst into a tremendous sunny smile. So I decided he couldn't be so sick after all."

———————◆———————

The journey by train from coastal Maine to New York City was long and slow. There was plenty of time for FDR to reflect on the frightening turn his life had taken.

A trauma like sudden paralysis tears the foundation out from under every ambition and plan. But few people had ambitions and plans as large as Franklin Roosevelt's.

For most of his life, he had pictured himself as a leader-in-the-making. Even his earliest memory, or so he claimed, was of a torchlight parade that trundled past his family's home on the night that Governor Grover Cleveland of New York, a friend of his father's, was elected president of the United States. Before long he imagined that he himself might become the sort of man who could inspire that sort of celebration.

But he was not a born leader. When he was thirteen, the age when many boys of his social class went away to boarding school, his mother kept him at home for an extra year. So when she finally sent him off to Groton, a school near Boston, he got a late start in making friends and never quite caught up. Franklin was sometimes invited to visit the home of Theodore Roosevelt and play with his five children. But that exuberant crew whispered that Franklin was a bit of a sissy. He was good at sailing and golf, but in the top-tier sports of football and baseball, he never made the team. He was the kind of kid who always seemed to be trying a little too hard to be popular. At Harvard College he was chosen to be president of the school newspaper, the *Crimson*, but he failed to win an invitation to join the most prestigious social club, Porcellian, a slight that left him deeply disappointed.

At last, in college, he did make some close friends. They were the ones who heard him voice his great ambition. "I can remember so well sitting out with him at a party," one said later, "and he was perfectly definite about so many things for the future, and he said, 'I know I want to try for the presidency of the United States.'"

The example of his distant cousin Theodore towered in his mind. Franklin's parents had always looked down on the common run of politicians as rough and corrupt men. But "Cousin Theodore" broke that mold. T.R., as he was known, had proven that a man of their own class—a true "gentleman"— could battle for good in the public arena without using dirty tactics. As Sara once put it, T.R. showed that a gentleman could "go into politics but not *be* a politician." When FDR was about to leave for Harvard, his uncle Fred had suggested he read a speech by his "noble kinsman," who urged well-to-do young Americans like Franklin to embrace "the strenuous life." T.R. had declared, "Far better it is to dare mighty things, to win glorious triumphs, even though checkered by failure, than to take rank with those poor spirits who neither enjoy much nor suffer much, because they live in the gray twilight that knows not victory nor defeat."

Theodore had started as a crusading reformer in politics, cleaning up the police department in New York City and fighting corrupt political bosses in the state capital of Albany. At the same time he wrote popular books about American history and his own adventures as a hunter and cowboy in the Dakotas. Next, as assistant secretary of the U.S. Navy, he took a hand in launching a war with Spain. Just a few months later, he led a cavalry squadron called the Rough Riders against the Spanish army in Cuba. Welcomed home as a war hero in 1898, he was promptly elected governor of New York. Two years later he became vice president of the United States. And when President William McKinley was shot dead by an assassin in 1901, Theodore assumed the presidency.

Until then, Franklin had admired his older cousin from a distance. They knew each other, but not very well. That changed in 1903, when Franklin proposed marriage to Eleanor Roosevelt, the president's favorite niece and Franklin's own fifth cousin once removed. FDR loved Eleanor. There was no doubt of that. But it's hard not to suspect that he also enjoyed the prospect of forging a closer tie through marriage to the president of the United States. In 1905—after a long engagement, which Franklin's mother had insisted on, and two years in law school at Columbia University—the two young representatives of different branches of the extended Roosevelt clan were married in a big "society wedding" in New York City. Relatives and friends looked on as the president, up from Washington, escorted the bride down the aisle. Her name remained what it had always been—Anna Eleanor Roosevelt.

As president, Theodore Roosevelt built the Panama Canal, fought the power of overgrown corporations, started the national park system, and hunted grizzly bears for fun. He was a Republican. Franklin's branch of the family were Democrats. But Franklin hung a portrait of Theodore next to a portrait of his father. The difference in political parties didn't matter. He wanted a life like that of the man he now called Uncle Ted.

Another friend remembered Franklin saying that he planned to follow T.R.'s example step-by-step. First he would run for the New York state legislature. Then, again like Uncle Ted, he would go to Washington as assistant secretary of the navy. Next: governor of New York—"and anyone who is governor of New York has a good chance to be president," he said.

Many people, when they're young, spin visions of a grand future. Most of them find out it's a lot easier to dream about doing great things than it is to actually do them. So they put their dreams away and settle for less.

It was different with Franklin Roosevelt.

By 1921, he had taken two of the steps marked out by T.R.—serving in the New York legislature, then as assistant secretary of the navy. He had even been nominated for vice president, like T.R., though the older Roosevelt had won his election to that post, while FDR had lost his race in 1920.

At the start of his career he'd not been a natural politician, just as he'd not been a natural leader in school. Politics rewards people who can make friends with practically anybody, from street cleaners and farmers to judges and senators. As a rookie state senator at age twenty-eight, FDR felt at home on the upper rungs of society's ladder, but not the lower. And he had to learn that in politics, even an idealist had to give a little to get things done.

In Albany he met a gifted young political activist named Frances Perkins, who was urging legislators to pass a law to limit the hours of working women. In time the two would become close friends and colleagues. But in their early meetings, Perkins thought FDR was stuck-up, and so did others. Perkins remembered a friendly old senator named Tim Sullivan saying: "Awful arrogant fellow, that Roosevelt."

She described the young FDR at work in the state senate, "tall and slender, very active and alert . . . rarely talking with the members, who more or less avoided him, not particularly charming (that came later), artificially serious of face, rarely smiling, with an unfortunate habit—so natural that he was unaware of it—of throwing his head up. This, combined with his pince-nez [glasses] and great height, gave him the appearance of looking down his nose at most people." She recalled him facing off with a couple of older senators who were "arguing with him to be 'reasonable,' as they called it, about something." But he tossed that chin up and in "his cool, remote voice" said, "No, no, I won't hear of it!"

Ten years in politics and government rubbed off the arrogance. In the state senate he had been trying too hard to be serious and "senatorial." But even then, Frances Perkins said, he loved to laugh. Gradually he relaxed into a political style more in line with his natural warmth and humor. Meanwhile, Louis Howe helped him learn the tactics needed to get things done and advance his own prospects.

It wasn't easy.

He made his name in the state senate by fighting the powerful men who ran the Democratic Party in giant New York City. The local Democratic organization was known by the name of its headquarters, Tammany Hall. The bosses of Tammany were mostly Irish Americans whose ancestors had been snubbed by New York's elite for generations. Through politics they had grabbed a share of power, and often they used it for personal gain. The "Tammany machine," it was called—a political factory where elections were rigged and corrupt deals were hatched.

When the current boss of Tammany Hall, "Silent Charlie" Murphy, tried to put one of his pals in the U.S. Senate, Roosevelt led the idealistic reformers who quashed the scheme. That earned him a big black mark in Tammany's ledger. When he tried to make his own run for the U.S. Senate in 1914, the Tammany machine slapped him down. He had to face the fact that if he was ever to run for statewide office, he would have to make peace with Tammany.

So by quiet signals he let the bosses know that while he would never play the game their way, neither would he make them his target.

He also learned that politics was not a simple matter of good and evil. With experience, he saw that Tammany politicians often did more practical good—giving food to poor families in trouble, helping the jobless find work—than high-minded reformers who talked about helping the oppressed people of the earth but didn't actually know any.

One of those politicians was Tim Sullivan, the state senator who had found the young Roosevelt so arrogant. Born in the poor and violent Irish American neighborhood called Five Points, Sullivan had come up from shining shoes and selling newspapers to owning saloons, vaudeville theaters, and race-tracks. Then he'd joined the Tammany machine, which sent him to the state assembly, the state senate, and the U.S. House of Representatives. Sullivan took payoffs and traded political favors for votes. He also gave new shoes by the thousand to destitute people in his district. Knowing the everyday dangers of the city's slums, he pushed through the state's first law against carrying concealed weapons. When Frances Perkins was fighting for shorter hours for working women, Roosevelt opposed her. So did the Tammany legislators in Albany—except Tim Sullivan, whose sister had gone to work in a factory at fourteen to help her family.

FDR got to know Sullivan. Later on, when Franklin had become a firm supporter of women's rights, he told Frances Perkins, "Tim Sullivan used to say that the America of the future would be made out of the people who had come over in steerage [emigrated from Europe to the United States in the worst quarters of passenger ships] and who knew in their own hearts and lives the difference between being despised and being accepted and liked.

"Poor old Tim Sullivan never understood about modern politics. But he was right about the human heart."

———————◆———————

FDR's cousin Joseph Alsop later said that after the 1920 election, Roosevelt "looked remarkably like another specimen of a familiar American political type—the attractive young man who makes politics his profession, comes up fast at first, and then runs into a dead end and spends the rest of his life regretting former glories that everyone else soon forgets."

FDR had no intention of letting that happen.

First, he laid plans to support his family by earning more money than he had been able to make in his ten years of government service. He wanted to supplement the handouts from his mother, perhaps even make them unnecessary. So he joined Langdon Marvin, his old friend from Harvard, in a New York law firm that was promptly renamed Emmet, Marvin & Roosevelt. At the same time he accepted a job offer from Van Lear Black, whose businesses included the Fidelity & Deposit Company, an insurance firm; Black wanted FDR to run the New York office. In both cases—the law firm and the insurance company—it was understood that Roosevelt would be a part-timer. His main value lay in the prestige of having the name Roosevelt on the door. His associates knew he would be devoting much of his time to politics.

He wasn't running for anything yet. That would happen at some point down the road—just when was hard to say. After eight years in Washington, his job right now was to get back into New York's political ecosystem. He looked out for trusted assistants who had worked for him at the Navy Department and on the 1920 campaign, so that when the next campaign came, he could bring them back on board. He arranged for jobs for several of them, including Louis Howe, who went to work for Fidelity & Deposit, and Marguerite LeHand, who became his full-time secretary. (She soon was so close to the Roosevelt family that the children began to call her "Missy," and the nickname stuck.)

FDR didn't talk about his long-term intentions, not with anyone but Howe. But hints slipped out now and then. When a deeply loyal booster named Tom

Lynch couldn't get past his disappointment over Roosevelt's defeat in the race for vice president, FDR counseled him to be patient.

"Tom," he said, "1932 will be our year."

Now any such hopes depended on his legs. If his strength returned, if he could stand up and walk again, he could get back on the track he had set for himself.

If not, his future was lost.

———————•◆•———————

From Grand Central Terminal in New York, FDR was driven to Presbyterian Hospital, then carted up to a private room for several more weeks of rest. His personal physician, Dr. George Draper, had taken charge of the case. After a brief examination of his patient, Dr. Draper would meet with reporters demanding news about the famous young politician.

It was good for FDR to have a man like Draper on his side. They had known each other since Groton School. Dr. Draper was smart and serious about his work. He had been a physician in the U.S. Army during World War I. (In fact, he still looked like a strict army officer, with a narrow face, a high forehead, and piercing eyes.) He knew perhaps as much about polio as Dr. Lovett did, since he had treated many patients in the 1916 epidemic and studied the disease in the years since then. He didn't have time to examine Roosevelt carefully before he met with reporters that day, but otherwise he was well prepared to answer their questions.

The earliest news reports about FDR's illness had been muddled. So it was up to Dr. Draper to tell everyone the truth.

He did—mostly.

Hard as it was to believe, he said, the vigorous politician of the 1920 campaign had come down with infantile paralysis. For the time being, Roosevelt was unable to walk.

But there was good news, too.

"Power is already beginning to return to the affected muscles," Dr. Draper said, "and this is a promising sign. His general condition is exceedingly good and he is in the best of spirits."

What about the future? the reporters asked. Would Roosevelt be permanently paralyzed?

"I can say definitely that he will not be crippled," Dr. Draper declared, "and no one should have any fear of permanent injury in any way from this attack."

Like Dr. Lovett, Dr. Draper knew perfectly well that it was too early to make that promise. No doctor could predict whether FDR's muscles would recover a lot or a little or not at all.

So why would he say that?

Probably because he wanted his patient to read it in the next day's newspapers.

For a physician of his era, Dr. Draper had some unusual ideas. In his own lifetime, scientists had made huge strides in understanding the causes of disease. But Dr. Draper believed the human body still concealed imponderable mysteries.

He thought it wasn't enough for a doctor to know which germ could be killed by which medication. A lot depended on the patients—their upbringings, their immune systems, even their minds. Draper urged his fellow doctors to study their patients' personalities. Too many doctors had lost track of "the powerful agencies of faith and hope," he wrote. If he had two patients with exactly the same physical problem but different attitudes toward that problem, he believed the patient who was fighting for a comeback stood a much better chance than the patient who gave up in despair.

Dr. Draper wanted FDR to hope for what Dr. Lovett had spoken of— "spontaneous improvement" in his damaged muscles. Maybe it would happen; maybe it wouldn't. But Draper wanted FDR to be in a fighting mood.

So the doctor spoke words to the reporters that he knew FDR would read in the newspapers. The words set a goal: "He will not be crippled."

An able-bodied person like Dr. Draper could *talk* about what it's like to be paralyzed. But only someone who is actually paralyzed really knows.

It was bad enough that FDR couldn't get up and walk, let alone run or play sports or drive a car. But it was a lot worse than simply losing those abilities.

Some paralyzed people can't control the muscles needed to go to the bathroom. If so, they have to use tubes called catheters that carry waste out of the body. FDR had needed a catheter right at first, but in this one small way he was lucky. In his case, those muscles regained their strength in just a few weeks. But he still needed help when he had to urinate or defecate.

In fact, he needed a helper nearby day and night. When he wanted to eat, someone had to bring him food. When he wanted to read a book, someone had to fetch it from the shelf. He couldn't change his clothes without assistance. If he were to fall, he would stay on the floor until someone came. If there were a fire, he couldn't escape by himself. So he could never enjoy total solitude and privacy. He may have felt as many people feel when paralyzed—like an infant in the body of an adult.

A historian named Daniel Wilson, who had polio himself, talked to many men who, like FDR, had been struck by polio as adults. "In their own eyes," Wilson wrote, "and often in the attitudes and words of their nurses and attendants, they had been reduced to the condition of babies. Like babies, they could do little for themselves, but they never completely lost their sense of manhood, and the incongruity between their treatment and a sense of self added to their pain."

When you're paralyzed, even loved ones begin to treat you differently, as if you are some strange new person they hardly know. People who talk to you, even good friends, don't know what to say. After polio struck FDR, a friend of the family couldn't even compose a letter to Eleanor. "I have tried hard to write you," she finally explained after months of delay, "but I simply did not know how to express my feelings."

People with permanent paralysis seldom want their loved ones to know how frightened they feel. Many cover up their feelings with jokes and cheerfulness that's only half-sincere. FDR did that a lot, and Eleanor knew it. She once wrote: "There were certain things that he never really talked about—that he would just shut up, and it made him very, very much alone in some ways."

———◆———

The normal and natural thing to do in this situation is simply to say, "Well, I guess I have to live with this for a while, but it's only going to be temporary. I'll get over it."

That's exactly what Dr. Draper had told the reporters. So that's what FDR said to everyone in the letters he dictated while lying on his back in his hospital bed.

"I am well ahead of the record-breaking schedule I have set out to maintain in recovery," he wrote to a good friend in Hyde Park. To a friend in Washington, D.C., he wrote: "I am still just as much of an optimist as ever, and I appear to have inspired the doctors with a certain amount of optimism as well, as they are most encouraging as to the future."

It was the same with visiting relatives and friends. A reporter who talked to several of them later remarked that "Roosevelt gaily brushed aside every hint of condolence and sent them away more cheerful . . . None of them heard him utter a complaint or a regret or even acknowledge that he had had so much as a bit of hard luck." When his old boss at the Navy Department, Josephus Daniels, came to FDR's bedside, Roosevelt threw a playful punch at Daniels's chest. "You thought you were coming to see an invalid!" he said with a laugh.

But in one joking letter from the hospital, there was a hint that he knew the truth might not be so rosy. FDR had just read an article in the *New York Times* about Dr. Draper's remarks to the press. He dictated a note to the famous publisher of the *Times*, Adolph Ochs, whom he knew.

"While the doctors were unanimous in telling me that the attack was very mild and that I was not going to suffer any permanent effects from it," he told Ochs, "I had, of course, the usual dark suspicion that they were just saying nice things to make me feel good, but now that I have seen the same statement officially made in the New York Times I feel immensely relieved because I know of course it must be so."

Chapter 4

"HE'S THROUGH"

Every day, Dr. Draper dropped by Presbyterian Hospital to see how his patient was doing.

Still too weak in his lower back to sit up, FDR would talk and talk and talk, telling Draper he planned to be up on crutches within a couple of weeks, leave the hospital, and then begin a hard program of exercise. He'd be walking on his own in no time.

As he chattered on, Dr. Draper would listen, all the while watching the movements of Roosevelt's arms and back, placing his hands on a muscle here and a muscle there, asking FDR to try moving this or that. The doctor had to be very gentle. It was now nearly two months since the poliovirus had struck, but many of FDR's muscles were still painfully tender.

Dr. Draper was looking for any signs that paralyzed muscles were coming back to life on their own. He was hoping that healthy nerve cells were starting to take up the slack for cells killed by the virus.

The doctor saw promising signals in the arms and chest. His patient could now hold a pen and sign his name to a letter. He could reach up and grasp a heavy strap over his bed and pull himself up so the nurses could change his sheets or give him a sponge bath. This gave FDR "a great sense of satisfaction," Draper noted. Still, certain muscles in the shoulders and arms remained weak.

Below FDR's chest, Dr. Draper saw only bad news. In the lower back and buttocks—essential for standing, walking, and sitting up—the muscles had withered. The legs, feet, and toes presented "a most depressing picture," Dr. Draper wrote to Dr. Lovett. FDR could make certain toes twitch just a little. But he couldn't move his feet. In his calves he could make a couple of muscles twitch, but nothing more. Above the knees, the virus had devastated the muscles of his thighs.

At Campobello, Dr. Lovett had told the Roosevelts to watch for signs of recovery in a couple of weeks. With the New York reporters, Dr. Draper had promised "he will not be crippled."

But if Dr. Draper had felt optimistic at first—partly because of what Dr. Lovett had said, no doubt—now he was not so sure.

He detected one especially frightening possibility. The muscles in FDR's lower back, critical to staying upright in a seated position, were too tender for Dr. Draper to examine carefully. But he suspected they were in very bad shape. He wrote about his concerns in a private letter to Dr. Lovett in Boston:

"He is very cheerful and hopeful, and has made up his mind that he is going to go out of the hospital in the course of two or three weeks on crutches. What I fear more than anything else is that we shall find a much more extensive involvement of the great back muscles than we have suspected and that when we attempt to sit him up he will be faced with the frightfully depressing knowledge that he cannot hold himself erect."

Dr. Draper was worried about more than FDR's paralysis. He was worried about his willpower.

FDR would have to endure a long, difficult, and painful program of exercise. To get through it, he must pin his hopes to the vision of a strong recovery. But if he discovered that he couldn't even sit up, how could he ever believe that he might walk again?

"I feel so strongly after watching him for over a week that the psychological factor in his management is paramount," Dr. Draper told Dr. Lovett. "He has such courage, such ambition, and yet at the same time such an extraordinarily sensitive emotional mechanism that it will take all the skill which we can master to lead him successfully to a recognition of what he really faces without utterly crushing him."

From this, it sounds as if Dr. Draper had begun to think that FDR's legs would never work again. If that turned out to be true, could he summon the courage to live his life without the ability to walk? Or would he give up in despair?

A few days later, on Dr. Lovett's advice, Dr. Draper had the nurses lower FDR into hot baths. The heat soothed his back muscles, and FDR did sit up. So he would not be imprisoned in a bed. It was a crucial success.

But below the waist, his legs were the same as ever.

———— • ◆ • ————

Sara Roosevelt was keeping herself "very cheerful," Eleanor noticed, though "it must have been a most terrific strain for her, and I am sure that, out of sight, she wept many hours."

At Campobello, Sara had tried to believe that Franklin would make a full recovery. But like her brother, Fred Delano, she had been raised to look hard facts in the face.

Now, in her son's hospital room, she could see what seemed the obvious truth: His legs simply were not getting any better. If he would never walk again, what should he do with his life?

To Sara the answer was quite clear. He should retire to the family's country home at Hyde Park. With her fortune, there was no need for him to worry about making a living. He could pursue his hobbies. He could add to his collections of books, fine art, and stamps. Perhaps he would write articles or even books. He loved Hyde Park. He could live out a pleasant life there in privacy.

So she left New York City to make preparations in the big house overlooking the Hudson.

While she was doing so, a friend of hers, Mrs. Lily Norton, visited for a few days and listened to Sara's story of all that had happened. Then Mrs. Norton sat down to write a letter to a friend. Her thoughts probably reflected what Sara had been thinking:

"Tragedy rather overshadows this once so happy & prosperous family, for Mrs. R's only son, Franklin Roosevelt, was struck down in August with a terribly serious case of infantile paralysis. He is only 39 . . . He's had a brilliant career . . . Now he is a cripple—will he ever be anything else? His mother is wonderfully courageous & plucky, but it's a bitter blow."

———— ◆ ————

When the news of FDR's illness appeared in the newspapers, his friends in politics were relieved to learn the doctors were predicting a full recovery. But as he stayed in the hospital week after week, they became curious about how he was really doing.

One of these friends was James Middleton Cox, a wealthy newspaper publisher who had been the governor of Ohio and FDR's running mate on the Democratic ticket in 1920. When he visited the hospital, Cox was shocked. He just couldn't believe that FDR, the athletic young man who had campaigned so vigorously just a year earlier, had been cut down by a child's disease.

"Jim's eyes filled with tears when he saw me," FDR recalled later, "and I gathered from his conversation that he was dead certain that I had had a stroke and that another one would soon completely remove me . . . Jim Cox from that day on always shook his head when my name was mentioned and said in sorrow that in effect I was a hopeless invalid and could never resume any active participation in business or political affairs."

Other visitors saw that FDR was nowhere near walking, and they passed that news to friends. Young Roosevelt was putting up a good front, they said. He was a brave fellow, all right. But as for politics, the Democrats could forget about him.

"The word had spread around," said Frances Perkins. It was: "'Poor Roosevelt, he's through.' 'Too bad about Roosevelt, he's through.' 'Too bad.'"

———————•◆•———————

Why would a man like James Cox cry at the mere sight of his friend?

Why would everyone think FDR was through in politics just because he couldn't walk?

Why would they think his life was ruined?

The reason was that many people of that era thought a physical disability was something to be ashamed of, even something repulsive. The common word for a disabled person was *cripple*, which implied that the person was not a whole and normal human being. To be crippled by polio seemed especially unpleasant. Like the Roosevelts themselves, their friends heard the words "infantile paralysis" and thought of children with horribly twisted arms and legs. It was an awful disease, and many people just didn't want to think about it.

Maybe they wouldn't say it out loud, but some still had wild notions that came out of the Middle Ages, when people with disabilities were thought to be children of the devil. Many took it for granted that disability was God's punishment for sins. The word for *cripple* in several languages came from the ancient word for *crawl*, since that was the only way severely disabled people of ancient times could move around. Even in the twentieth century, the idea lingered that a disabled person was like a crawling animal.

The treatment of disabled people had improved. But most disabled people in the 1920s lived lonely, boring lives, shut away in the homes of relatives. Very few could get jobs. Employers asked, Why hire a disabled man—let alone a disabled woman—over a non-disabled person, especially since people with disabilities were thought to be nervous, depressed, and unreliable?

So it was just a matter of common sense that a "crippled" man could never be a leader. People weren't even thinking about the sheer physical difficulty of moving around. Elect a crippled man to high office? It was as if someone thought a five-year-old should run for president. It just wasn't going to happen.

———— ◆ ————

In late October 1921, two months after the diagnosis of polio, Dr. Robert Lovett traveled from Boston to see firsthand how Roosevelt was doing. He and Dr. Draper discussed the case, then agreed the patient was ready to leave the hospital.

With that, Sara Roosevelt announced that the house at Hyde Park was ready and waiting. But she had a surprise coming.

No, Mama, her son said. (He gave it the upper-class English pronunciation *ma-MA*.) He would not be taking the train up to Hyde Park anytime soon, at least not for the reasons she had in mind. He was going straight back to East Sixty-Fifth Street, close to the doctors and nurses who would help him with his recovery program. He meant to start right away.

People who thought Franklin Roosevelt was a "mama's boy" would have learned something from that short conversation.

Uncle Fred had advised him to face facts and not fool himself.

But FDR had decided he was going to make his own facts.

———— ◆ ————

Louis Howe was thinking the same way.

In the months before FDR became ill, Howe had been pondering his own future. He had been working under Roosevelt at Fidelity & Deposit, but he was now weighing a couple of offers for better positions with bigger salaries. He felt the deepest loyalty to FDR. But in the wake of the polio attack, did it make sense to keep working for a politician who suddenly seemed to have no political future? Howe had his family to think of. But he would not make his decision until Roosevelt made a decision of his own.

As Howe told the story, the two men were talking one day when Howe remarked on the choice that FDR had to make.

FDR could do what his mother was proposing, Howe said. He could retire to Hyde Park, live the life of a quiet country invalid, tinkering with this project or that, writing on subjects that interested him, and give up any thought of a life in politics.

That would be perfectly all right, Howe said. It would be "a useful life engaged in literary work and other things that required no personal agility."

Or, he told FDR, "you can . . . gather up your courage and plunge forward as though nothing had happened." Maybe he could learn to walk again; maybe not. He would have to find ways to climb the stairs to railroad platforms, get in and out of automobiles, cross stages in front of thousands of people. He would risk embarrassment, maybe even ridicule.

If he wanted to do that, Howe said, "I will go along with you every inch of the hard way."

According to Howe, FDR did not hesitate. He flashed his giant grin and said, "Well, when do we begin?"

There is every reason to think FDR had made that decision already. He did not need Louis Howe to arouse his ambition.

———◆———

For Eleanor Roosevelt, her husband's decision meant she must abandon the work she wanted to do, or so it certainly seemed.

Soon after FDR's failed campaign for vice president in 1920, she had begun to work in politics herself. Women had just gained the right to vote, and Eleanor saw that many women needed encouragement to take a larger part in public affairs—to vote, to campaign for candidates, to organize supporters in favor of good laws and policies, even to run for office. She began to join committees and work for Democratic Party candidates in New York.

But now her husband's illness seemed to dominate everything. FDR wanted Louis Howe to move in with the family so he could help with FDR's recovery, his business affairs, and his political plans. So Eleanor would have to reorganize the whole household to make room for Howe. She would have to arrange all the details of hiring a live-in nurse and making appointments with doctors. Getting Franklin ready for a return to politics was going to be a full-time job. She would have less time than ever for her own projects.

That would be difficult enough, but the idea of retiring to Hyde Park seemed to Eleanor to be even worse. In Hyde Park, her mother-in-law ruled the roost. The estate there belonged to Sara, not her son. Eleanor loved her mother-in-law, but she resented Sara's efforts to dominate the family's life. Retirement to Hyde Park before Eleanor was even forty years old would mean consigning herself to a comfortable cage.

She went to Dr. Draper: What did *he* think of her husband's wish to return to politics?

Dr. Draper said he was all for it. Even if FDR didn't succeed in the long run, he told her, the effort would lift his spirits and improve his chance to make a strong physical recovery.

Eleanor agreed. Frances Perkins, now Eleanor's friend as well as Franklin's, said, "She thought he would die spiritually, die intellectually, and die in his personality, if he didn't have political hope."

As for her own hopes, Eleanor said much later, "I do not think I ever stopped to analyze my feelings. There was so much to do to manage the household and the children and to try to keep things running smoothly that I never had any time to think of my own reactions. I simply lived from day to day and got through the best I could."

She fit a new job into her crowded routine. In league with Louis Howe, she set about keeping FDR in touch with politics and government even as he lay in his bed. She clipped newspaper reports and editorials for him to read. She invited friends in politics to come to the house and fill him in on the latest news and gossip. She and Louis sat and talked with him by the hour.

———— ◆ ————

Sara Roosevelt could hardly believe what she was hearing.

It was absolutely crazy—a crippled man running for office? Like most people, she took it for granted that a man with a disability should remove himself from public view. If being crippled was not quite shameful, she thought, it was certainly something to be kept as private as possible. *Her* son, exhibiting himself with crippled legs before common people? Unable to go up a staircase unless two men carried him?

She insisted that he stop the nonsense. She became "quite vociferous in her demands," Anna remembered.

Sara went to Louis Howe. She disapproved of the little man, with his sour manners and his sloppy habits, but she respected his judgment. Surely, she said, Howe, with all his experience, must realize that FDR had no future in politics.

In fact, Louis told her, he still believed that one day her son would be president of the United States.

Finally FDR told his mother he had heard quite enough. She was not to speak of the matter again.

"Franklin had no intention of conforming to my quiet ideas for his future existence," Sara wrote later. "He was determined to ignore his disability and carry on from where he had left off."

He simply refused to voice any doubt of his ability to make a complete recovery. "He has never said he could not walk," Eleanor remarked later, and he wanted no one else in the family to say it, either. If he allowed himself to think for an instant that he might not reach his goal, then he might lose his courage and fall into despair.

Psychologists call this way of thinking *denial*. It means refusing to accept a fact that you just can't bear. It can get you in deep trouble. Usually it's best to face up to harsh truths, just as Uncle Fred had advised FDR.

But sometimes denial is a powerful tool that helps people do things no one else thinks they can do.

FDR knew very well that people privately made fun of him as a man spoiled and bossed around by his mother. His hard-charging Roosevelt cousins—Theodore Roosevelt's children—used to say his initials stood for *Feather Duster*. People said all the good things in life had been handed to him on a silver platter.

Now he'd been cut down by a disease that normally struck children. In every phase of his life, it seemed, somebody had whispered that he was a weakling.

So he just said no—no to the insults, no to his mother, no to polio.

He intended to show everybody who and what he really was.

PART 2

STANDING UP

· ·

NOVEMBER 1921– JULY 1924

Chapter 5

TRIAL AND ERROR

••••••••••••••••••••••••••••••

"When do we begin?" he had asked Louis Howe.

FDR wanted to start today, tomorrow—whenever the doctors gave the signal, if not sooner.

"The patient is doing very well," Dr. Draper wrote Dr. Lovett in November 1921. "[He] navigates about successfully in a wheel chair. He is exceedingly ambitious and anxious to get to the point where he can try the crutches."

For the time being, Dr. Draper insisted, more rest was essential.

But FDR wanted no more rest.

"I absolutely concur in your belief that a fellow 'can put anything across if he is game to tackle it,'" he wrote one friend. "I am trying out the theory myself, having determined to get well in the shortest possible time."

"I am still just as much of an optimist as ever," he declared.

He got an encouraging message from Joseph Tumulty, a powerful politician who had been chief of President Woodrow Wilson's staff in the White

House. FDR replied: "The doctors all predict a speedy and complete recovery for me. I hope not only to be back on the fighting line but to have a lot of highly spirited ammunition in the way of convincing arguments as to why one should be a Democrat."

When he talked like that, he was stretching the doctors' predictions well beyond what they had really said. True, Dr. Lovett had told FDR to expect some improvement in the first few weeks. But that was very different from saying he would make "a speedy and complete recovery." Dr. Lovett had said only that a complete recovery wasn't out of the question. FDR didn't hear it that way. He wanted progress by leaps and bounds.

Dr. Lovett's whole approach was the opposite of leaps and bounds.

The doctor was thinking about the microscopic landscape of FDR's muscles. Deep in the muscle tissue, some of FDR's nerve cells had been killed and would never come back to life. Others had survived the attack with no damage at all. They might be ready to take over the work of cells that had died. And still other cells had been sitting still for so long they'd gone to sleep—but they might wake up again.

Which cells were which? Right now, no one could tell. The only way to find out was to get FDR's legs moving.

It would be best if he could make the muscles move on his own. If he couldn't, a nurse could grasp his legs, one at a time, and move them.

But there was danger in overdoing it. A patient who rushed recovery from polio might wind up very sorry. Trying too much too soon could kill injured nerves that might have been saved. A patient who became exhausted might have to quit for a while. That would waste time and energy, and it might deflate the person's hopes.

So . . . go slow—that's what Dr. Lovett had learned in his years of treating polio patients in the gloomy months that trickled by after the virus had finally left the body.

Go slow . . . but *watch closely.* It was also possible to go *too* slowly.

Paralyzed limbs, if left alone, could bend and twist out of shape and stay that way.

The poliovirus attacks a bundle of muscles the way a tornado attacks a town. A tornado can leave one block of houses untouched, while it plows up a row of houses just one street over. It's the same with the virus. It leaves the nerves in one bunch of muscle fibers alone while it ruins the nerves in the fibers next door. Then, day after day and little by little, the healthy muscles pull against the dead muscles. After weeks or months, the victim notices—though it seems unbelievable—that the paralyzed limb is actually changing from its normal shape or getting stuck in an extended position. Doctors call this a *contracture.*

It can happen in the toes, ankles, knees, hips. Even the spine can curve under the pressure of a contracture. A contracture can be prevented, but only by encasing the body part in casts and braces. It's also possible to reverse a contraction after it develops, but that takes a hard operation—more pain, more time, more suffering.

So *go slow* and *watch closely* were Dr. Lovett's strict instructions—not just to FDR but to Kathleen Lake, the no-nonsense nurse who first knocked on the Roosevelts' door in early December 1921.

Mrs. Lake had worked for Dr. Lovett and his patients many times before. She knew all about polio, and she practiced the new medical specialty called physiotherapy. This was a method for teaching people with injured limbs to move as well as they possibly could. It was hard, slow, exacting work for the patient and the nurse alike.

Mrs. Lake knew just how to do it. Day after day, dressed in a starched white uniform, she got down to business with her famous new patient.

———— ◆ ————

First, Mrs. Lake and a young woman named Edna Rockey, FDR's live-in nurse, would lift and haul the patient onto a long wooden board set up in his bedroom. With dark humor, FDR began to call that room "the Morgue."

During the long weeks when he had been lying and sitting still, some of his unused muscles had started to stick to each other. These points of stickiness are called *adhesions*. Another man who had polio remembered what it was like to tear adhesions apart, even by so simple a movement as being helped to sit up in his bed. "The least deflection of my limbs from the horizontal produced intense, exquisite pain," he wrote. "I had not been aware, until I was moved, just how painful and sensitive my body still was, nor did I expect the extreme fatigue that overcame me."

Now, every day, FDR began to go through that kind of pain.

Once he was in position on the long board, Mrs. Lake would give orders.

Move your left big toe, she would say.

He would try. Nothing would happen.

Try again, she would say. Again, he would strain just to twitch a muscle in the toe. Still nothing.

"Try it again."

"Try again."

"Again."

She wasn't being cruel. She knew it might take a hundred tries before a sleeping muscle moved, and if it moved once, it might move a second time. Then blood would start to flow through the muscle, and the whole toe might start to revive. If he could move one toe, he might be able to move one foot, and so on, but only with mind-numbing repetition. And there was no guarantee that one bit of progress would lead to more progress.

FDR was hoping for massage. It just seemed natural that rubbing and kneading the muscles would wake them up. But Dr. Lovett had forbidden any massage until the patient was free of pain. Later, massage could do some good. But at this stage, it could overwork and damage muscles just starting to recover.

Day by day, Mrs. Lake studied each of FDR's limbs as he struggled to do the exercises. She thought his left leg—the weaker of the two since the attack—was getting a bit stronger. But she also thought contractures might be forming in the hamstrings, the big muscles in the back of the thighs. So she and Nurse Rockey bent FDR's legs at the knees over and over, stretching the hamstrings to keep the legs from curling out of their normal shape.

So it went, testing and watching and working every muscle, not just below the waist but in the arms and hands, too, and in the abdomen and lower back.

Above the waist, Mrs. Lake saw real progress. FDR was doing many pull-ups with his overhead straps every day. While his lower body shriveled, his chest, shoulders, and upper arms were gaining new bulk and new strength. By the first week of January 1922, Mrs. Lake wrote to Dr. Lovett: "A friend of his told me he wouldn't have believed he was the same man he saw in November."

"He is a wonderful patient," Mrs. Lake wrote, "very cheerful & works awfully hard & tries every suggestion one makes to help him."

But then she became suspicious.

As January turned to February, she noticed that FDR would seem to make progress for a day or two. Then she would arrive the next morning to find the patient tired and cranky, with his ankles strangely swollen.

She called in Dr. Draper and told him what was happening.

Have you been overworking the patient? Draper asked.

Absolutely not, Mrs. Lake replied.

They were puzzled.

So Mrs. Lake did "a little private detective work" with Nurse Rockey, who attended FDR at night, when Mrs. Lake was gone.

Mrs. Lake asked the nurse if Mr. Roosevelt had been exercising at night.

Yes, he had, Miss Rockey replied.

"She remarked with some pride," Mrs. Lake wrote Dr. Lovett, "that she was doing some 'quite heavy manipulation' (her own words) on the patient at night."

Mrs. Lake went straight back to FDR, who admitted under questioning that he had asked Nurse Rockey to administer heavy Swedish massage to his legs—"to build up the muscles!" he told her. This was exactly the sort of deep-muscle massage the doctors had forbidden.

Mrs. Lake scolded him. Didn't he remember that massage could damage his fragile muscles at this point? He *must* take things slowly. Didn't he want to learn how to walk with crutches? He would never do so if he overworked his muscles.

Of course, he said. He was sorry.

"I am getting on extremely well," he wrote a friend just then, "though it seems slow, and I am not out of the house yet. However, as complete and permanent recovery is promised in a few months I am not worrying."

———————◆———————

Dr. Lovett came from Boston again. He saw something Mrs. Lake had missed. Yes, as she feared, FDR was developing contractures in the hamstring muscles. But Lovett also saw that where the legs met the upper body, muscles were hardening into contractures that could leave FDR permanently bent at the waist.

So Lovett brought in a specialist, Dr. Arthur Krida, who encased Roosevelt in rock-hard plaster casts from his waist to his ankles, one for each leg, with hinges at the joints.

Now FDR had to lie on his bed with his lower body absolutely rigid, twenty-four hours a day. Every day, Dr. Krida came back to the house. Every day, he would pound wedges into the joints of the casts. The farther he pounded the wedge, the more the contracting muscles stretched.

With no way to exercise his legs, FDR's fears rose to the surface. He asked Mrs. Lake, *With all this time lying still, won't I lose all the strength I've regained?*

For two weeks he lay entombed in the plaster casts. Finally Dr. Krida cut them off. The muscles had stretched. The danger of contracture was past, and the patient had not lost much strength.

Now, Dr. Lovett said, it was time to get Roosevelt up on his feet. The next goal was to learn the difficult art of walking with crutches.

———————————◆———————————

Of all the mammals, only humans stand upright on two feet. It is one of the traits that define us as a species. It seems easy to most of us only because we're used to it. We learned it as toddlers. But we forget the weeks of trial and error.

The apparently simple act of standing is actually a highly complicated effort requiring the coordination of nerves, muscles, and bones. The brain of a person getting up from a chair sends millions of signals through the motor nerves to the toes, feet, ankles, calves, thighs, buttocks, lower back, and abdomen, all the muscles moving in harmony to keep one hundred or two hundred pounds safely balanced on two loosely jointed stalks. The muscles have to be loose and limber enough to allow the legs to bend at the ankles, knees, hips, and waist—then strong enough to tighten in an instant, holding the bones in a straight line, locked at the joints.

Paralysis in any of the complex muscles of the legs makes this a mess.

That's how it was with FDR. The doctors and nurses tried once or twice to get him upright. But his knees and ankles simply collapsed under his weight.

So back came Dr. Krida to the house on East Sixty-Fifth Street. He took careful measurements of FDR's legs, ankles, and feet. In a few days he returned with a set of metal braces that weighed about ten pounds apiece. The braces were fastened to FDR's legs with leather straps and metal buckles. They extended from just above his waist down to his heels, with hinges at the knees. When the hinges were locked, FDR's whole lower body was held as stiff and straight as a tree trunk.

The nurses lifted him to his feet. They inserted a crutch under each armpit. With a nurse on each side, he stood up for the first time in half a year.

It was strangely frightening to attempt this feat, once so simple. Another young man recovering from polio—a less severe case than FDR's, with only one leg paralyzed—wrote: "It depressed me to find it so difficult . . . I had not known that the weakness of my hips, only slightly involved, would so completely destroy my feeling of security. Even with my back to a wall, my brace locked at the knee, I would feel brittle and vulnerable, at least ten feet tall; thinking that if I fell I would shatter on the floor like a tower of blocks."

FDR wouldn't shatter, but falls were definitely dangerous, especially with braces. Typically, a person who starts to fall goes into a quick crouch, bending at the knees to cushion the impact. Not so with FDR. If he went down, he would go *straight* down, like a tree sawed through at the ground.

He practiced just standing up with the braces holding his legs straight, trying to keep his balance. Then he began to make jerky stiff-legged movements across the floor, just a few inches at a time. Sometimes he would start to fall. The nurses would catch him and lift him back up. He would try again and fall again. It was the only way to learn how to do it. It was "a bizarre . . . system of muscular checks and balances that could not be taught," wrote a man who went through the same ordeal. "The body had to learn this on its own through days and days of trial and error."

When Mrs. Lake was away, FDR was supposed to rest. Instead, he often kept exercising. When she returned, he would talk at length about the methods he was thinking up. "He has all sort of new ideas for developing his muscles," Mrs. Lake told Dr. Lovett, "and I have to discourage him periodically, as tactfully as possible, otherwise he does considerably more harm than good."

"Counsel him not to try new methods," Lovett replied, "but to trust us to give him the maximum dose that he can stand for . . . He cannot be too careful."

But in his own mind, FDR disagreed. He *could* be too careful. Caution would never get him where he wanted to go.

As the winter of 1922 turned to spring, he was still telling friends he would be back in action very soon. He said his hips had recovered their normal strength, but he had less and less power the farther down his legs the muscles went, with about 15 percent of his normal strength in his toes. Still, he said, he was "gaining very surely."

"This foolish infantile paralysis germ has not destroyed any of the muscles," he told a friend, "and they are all coming back."

Dr. Draper saw things differently.

"He is walking quite successfully [with crutches and braces]," he wrote to Dr. Lovett, "and seems to be gaining power in the hip muscles. The quadriceps are coming a little, but they are nothing to brag of yet. Below the knee I must say it begins to look rather hopeless . . ."

Chapter 6

"EVERY AMERICAN STANDS"

Dr. Lovett suspected FDR "was going ahead a little too fast mentally." Once again he wanted to see the patient firsthand, and he wanted him to spend time with his associate, Wilhelmine Wright, a pioneer in physiotherapy. So he asked FDR to make the trip to Boston from New York.

Roosevelt jumped at the invitation. He told a close friend that Dr. Lovett "wants me for about ten days in Boston to get the right kind of braces made and to have his famous Miss Wright teach me how to walk better, so I will be more independent during the summer."

Wilhelmine Wright knew more than anyone in the world about how people with paralyzed limbs could regain the ability to move around. She had developed her methods year after year in her work with children and young adults recovering from polio. When it came to the basic skills of mobility, FDR was barely in kindergarten. Wright would put him through school.

Her method was to take the standard ways of getting around—standing up and sitting down, walking with crutches, going up and down stairs—and break them into small steps, each of them manageable if the patient would only think of them as isolated movements. Each step required practice and mastery. Then the steps could be merged into sustained mobility.

For a person in FDR's condition, standing up had to be done like this:

You're sitting in a heavy chair with arms, preferably a chair with its back pressed up against a wall. Your paralyzed legs are straight out in front of you. They're locked in braces so you can't bend at the knees. You hitch yourself up to the edge of the seat. Then, using both hands, you pick up your right leg and lift it across your left leg. Twisting hard to your left at the waist, you reach around to grab the arms of the chair with both hands. Then you flip your whole body around so that you're in a push-up position against the chair. From there, Wright said, "it is an easy matter to push the hips back and straighten the body while balancing with the chair, and finally to place one crutch and then the other under the arms."

Not *that* easy, maybe, but if you can manage it, you've stood up by yourself.

Standing upright, the patient could begin to learn how to walk with crutches. This was not easy at all. In fact, Wilhelmine Wright said crutch-walking with paralyzed legs was no easier than ice-skating or dancing, and like those activities, it took serious practice to do it well. (She knew boys who could speed along a city sidewalk just on crutches, without their feet touching the ground, then whip both legs and one crutch out to the side while spinning around a corner on the tip of the other crutch—an acrobatic feat that a gifted gymnast might be proud of.)

For the beginner, the method depended on how much strength you had above the waist. If you were weak in the shoulders, you had to use a slow, awkward "rocking chair" style of walking. For someone like Roosevelt, who was strong in the upper body, a better strategy was to swing the crutches out in front, then pull the legs forward with a little hop. This was faster and more graceful than the rocking-chair approach, but it still required careful coordination of arms and legs.

The hardest thing was to get up and down steps. A strong handrail was essential. You placed one crutch on the step in front of you, holding it steady with your armpit. You slid your other hand up the rail. Then you pushed up on the crutch side while pulling forward with the hand on the rail. That was one step. A typical staircase had thirteen more.

Miss Wright prescribed exercises, too—dozens of them.

For ten days FDR learned. Miss Wright was even more demanding than Mrs. Lake. If she said, "Do this," and he said, "I can't," she replied, "You never have before, but you are going to."

Dr. Lovett looked in from time to time. At the end of ten days he thought his patient was doing rather well. Confidentially, he wrote to Sara Roosevelt: "I wanted to get hold of him alone and observe him and see whether I thought he had been persistently overdoing at home . . . as in this way I thought I could control him better. Miss Wright has been able to teach him new tricks about walking and managing himself which have increased his confidence. I have made some changes to his braces, which I think will add to their efficiency, and he is really a good deal better and walks much better than he did when he came."

Dr. Lovett's goal for his patient was the same as it had been for some time—to walk well with crutches.

FDR's own goal was also unchanged. He intended to walk well *without* crutches.

———————◆———————

When FDR first got home from the hospital, Anna remembered years later, it was "the beginning of a period of adjustment to an entirely new life for the whole family."

At fourteen, she and her father were close. They had tramped the woods together at Hyde Park, gone riding on horseback, skated on the Hudson, swum at Campobello, always talking and joking. The realization that he was paralyzed shook her world. "I gradually grew accustomed to a new relationship with Father—a relationship where I had to go to his room and sit on a chair or at the foot of his bed when I wanted to talk to him. For some months my knowledge that he was suffering made me shy with him. But gradually his gaiety, his ability to poke fun at himself as he learned to move himself around through the use of his arms, broken down the tension we had been feeling." When she overheard rumors at school that his disease had affected his mind, she was outraged. She had no idea her father's political adversaries might spread such ideas just to hurt his chances of a comeback. "I did know, however, that the rumors were untrue," she wrote later. "I watched his courage, his suffering, his humor. I learned fast that he wanted no maudlin sympathy."

Instead, he dealt with the children's fears by bringing them into his confidence and telling them all about his effort to recover. He would invite them to his bedside and show them the depleted muscles in his legs, naming each one and explaining what he was doing to build them back up. The tactic worked. It chased away the children's sense of dread. "He would shout with glee over a little movement of a muscle that had been dormant," Anna said. "So, gradually, I almost forgot that he had once had well-developed muscles. The battle Father was making became a spirited game." With the boys he would drop to the floor and challenge them to wrestling matches.

Still, the family's focus had shifted entirely to one person—FDR himself—and the children's longings for him and their mother to pay attention to their own activities often went unmet.

Even before polio, the Roosevelts' family life had not been idyllic. The marriage had nearly broken apart when Eleanor learned that Franklin had conducted a love affair with Eleanor's secretary during World War I. The Roosevelts decided to stay together, but FDR's faithlessness had wounded Eleanor, and their relationship had been badly strained. She began to put more time into activities of her own, helping women and working people. Then, in the early days after the polio attack, her devotion to his care brought them closer again, though they seemed perhaps more like an adult brother and sister than husband and wife.

As for the children, they sensed the change in their parents' relations without knowing the reason. But that was just the latest development in their hectic history.

Eleanor had always been anxious about being a parent. Though she'd been born into privilege, she'd grown up in a tragic household. Her mother, Anna, renowned in New York society circles as a great beauty, was selfish, even nasty. Because Eleanor as a little girl was so serious-minded, her mother called her "Granny." Then Anna died of diphtheria when Eleanor was only eight. The child idolized her charming father, Theodore Roosevelt's brother Elliott, but he was an alcoholic who alternately adored and neglected her, then killed himself just two years after his wife's death. So her parents had been anything but models of good parenting.

As a teenager Eleanor blossomed at boarding school in England, where a brilliant and loving headmistress nurtured her intelligence and ability. But then, without attending college, at the age of just twenty, she married Franklin—and fell under the stern and constant gaze of her mother-in-law.

Eleanor read progressive advice about modern parenting and concluded that her children needed to be given a long leash and allowed to make their own mistakes. FDR largely agreed, remembering how aggravated he'd been by a mother who had directed his every move.

But their permissive style of parenting had its downside, especially because Sara often undermined their efforts by giving her grandchildren treats after they'd been disciplined. The kids grew up pretty wild. On Sixty-Fifth Street, James and Anna practiced their aim with bags of water dropped on passersby from the upper-story windows, and Elliott once tried to shoot out stained-glass windows across the street with his air rifle. Then there was a string of badly chosen governesses—young women who supervised the children when their mother was busy. One of them locked the boys in closets and once sent Anna to school with a wad of cotton stuffed in her mouth, saying the cotton had better be there when Anna came home at the end of the day. (She was finally fired only after Eleanor discovered she'd been drinking whiskey on the job.)

When polio invaded the household, Eleanor had to reengineer the daily schedule to accommodate FDR's work with nurses and doctors. Anna was forced to give up her bedroom when Louis Howe moved into the house every Monday through Friday. (Howe's own wife and two children now saw him only on weekends, thus making their own sacrifice to Franklin Roosevelt's needs.) It would be years before the children came to recognize any good traits in the sloppy, crotchety Howe, and they resented the friendship that grew between Howe and their mother. Sara Roosevelt, still astonished by her son's decision to try for a political comeback and afraid that his life was still in danger long after the poliovirus had left his body, was free with objections and arguments. In icily polite exchanges, she and Eleanor waged daily warfare over Franklin, the children, Howe (whom Sara detested), and just about everything else. If the children brought complaints to FDR, he would say, "That's up to Granny and Mother. You settle all this with them."

He still loved his wife and he certainly loved his children. But he put his battle against paralysis above everything else. In this Franklin was not so different from many American fathers of his time. He saw his role in the family as that of a chief executive. He would make the big decisions about money and household arrangements, which schools the children would attend and how they would spend their summers. But as for the children's day-to-day well-being, that was for his wife and mother to worry about. He hated to dole out punishment, even when the children deserved it. When he was paying attention to them, he was loads of fun. But he seems not to have thought very hard about what each of them really needed from him. "When we did have him,"

James wrote later, "life was as lively and exciting as any kid could want it to be." But even in the children's early years, he said, "we had so little of Father."

Now, during the fight of his life, they would have even less of him.

————— ◆ —————

When FDR returned to New York from Boston in the spring of 1922, the family began to make plans for spending the summer together, either in Hyde Park or perhaps at an oceanside cottage in Newport, Rhode Island. But the doctors had their own ideas.

Dr. Draper believed the endless arguments between Sara and Eleanor were driving his patient quietly nuts. FDR needed a break from "the interplay of those high-voltage personalities."

Dr. Lovett agreed. The best thing, he said, would be a few months of exercise with absolutely no distractions.

So FDR went up to the big estate at Hyde Park. He was accompanied only by Nurse Rockey and a full-time helper, LeRoy Jones, an African American man whom FDR called Roy.

Almost nothing is known of LeRoy Jones. He was one of many people the Roosevelts could afford to pay for doing the nitty-gritty work of daily life—cleaning, cooking, shopping, hauling, driving. In Jones's case, much of his job was even more intimate. He helped FDR get in and out of his clothes, right down to his underwear. He helped him in and out of chairs and his bed. He had to learn the delicate task of lowering FDR onto the toilet, then hoisting him off again, with FDR's hands encircling Jones's neck in a tight grip—a job he performed several times every day. For FDR that was one more loss to his sense of privacy and independence. What did it mean for LeRoy Jones? If others ever asked him, they made no record of what he said.

Once FDR was at Hyde Park, the family mostly stayed away. Louis Howe came for visits, as did a distant cousin invited by FDR's mother. Her name was Daisy Suckley (pronounced *SOOK-lee*), and in time she became one of FDR's closest friends.

The Roosevelts' estate at Hyde Park spread over many acres of lawn, field, and forest between the Albany Post Road—the old thoroughfare between New York City and the state capital—and the Hudson. The main house, built in stages from about 1800 to the 1910s, was more bulky than graceful, with squared-off rooflines and stubby chimneys. But for a big house it was inviting and comfortable. Tall windows afforded lovely views of the trees, the river, and the far shore. Inside the house, FDR knew every column and cupboard. Outside, he gazed on woods, slopes, and trails he had known since his boyhood.

All that summer and early fall of 1922, FDR exercised.

Indoors, he did pull-ups on his bed. Then he would sit at the bottom of a staircase, put his hands on the stair behind him, and hike himself up all the way to the top, stair by stair.

On the lawn, wearing his braces and a tight corset to keep from bending at the waist, he would stand between two parallel bars—one at waist level, the other at the height of his head—then reach forward and pull himself along from one end of the bars to the other, back and forth.

Often he would talk while he exercised. If his companion was Louis Howe, they would discuss politics and business. If it was Daisy Suckley, who had grown up and still lived in the nearby village of Rhinecliff, they would gossip about Hudson Valley relatives and friends.

She often heard him say, "I'm not going to be conquered by a childish disease."

---◆---

Week by week, the muscles of his neck, shoulders, arms, and chest swelled. Friends continued to be astonished at the new bulkiness of his body above the waist. In a letter, a navy friend who had seen a recent photo of FDR remarked that he appeared to be "passing from the Battle Cruiser to the Dreadnaught class."

"Don't worry about my getting fat," FDR replied. "The upper part of me weighs, of course, more than it did before, but that is because my arm and shoulder muscles have developed tremendously in the effort of getting about with crutches."

Actually, "getting about with crutches" was the one activity he seemed to be neglecting. Eleanor, who came to Hyde Park from time to time, and Nurse Rockey, who watched him every day, told Dr. Lovett the patient was slacking off on his crutch-walking exercises.

Lovett gave FDR a talking-to by mail, saying "walking on crutches is not a gift, but an art, acquired by constant practice."

FDR was all assurance, promising that "I have faithfully carried out all the walking."

But he really hadn't done so, and he didn't start. Within a few weeks, Nurse Rockey was sending Dr. Lovett her own tattletale letter. FDR was doing too much of the "mental work" the doctors had told him not to overdo, she said. If she didn't nag him, he would "make excuses and put off going to bed until very late, etc." When he did try his exercises with crutches, he wasn't ready for them. Just the other day, she said, "he was compelled to walk one-quarter of a mile, which completely took him off his feet for about four days." And his pain was back. "All this lovely fall has gone with only a few minutes devoted to walking," she said, "[and] not every day."

Why didn't he try harder to follow Dr. Lovett's orders?

The most likely answer is that the project of mastering crutch-walking simply didn't appeal to him, since crutches could never take him where he wanted to go.

FDR had been thinking hard about how to resume his quest for the presidency. Just as before his illness, he intended to start by running for a state-wide office in New York. But in his mind's eye, he simply could not imagine making such a campaign without the ability to stand and walk on his own.

In our time we've forgotten how important the simple act of standing up used to be for a man who considered himself a "gentleman," a term that was taken very seriously in the 1920s, especially in the Roosevelts' social class. In 1922, a writer named Emily Post was just launching her fabulously successful career as an expert on good manners with the publication of *Etiquette in Society, in Business, in Politics and at Home.* The book was full of advice about all the times when a well-behaved man must stand up. For example:

"A gentleman always rises when a lady comes into a room."

"In a restaurant, when a lady bows to him, a gentleman merely makes the gesture of rising by getting up half way from his chair and at the same time bowing. Then he sits down again."

"Every American citizen stands with his hat off at the passing of the 'colors' [the U.S. flag] and when the national anthem is played."

"If he gets on a street car . . . [h]e must not take a seat if there are ladies standing."

Yes, FDR could now be helped to a standing position. But it required something like what a football player requires to score a touchdown—hard physical effort, heavy equipment, and a lot of help from other people.

Then he would have to walk. To run for governor or senator, he would have to visit cities and towns all across the state of New York. Consider the movements necessary for him to deliver just one speech in some other city.

First, from his home on East Sixty-Fifth Street, he would need to get to a railroad platform at Grand Central Terminal. That would require an automobile. He couldn't possibly drive a car himself, so he would have to be chauffeured by a private car or a taxicab. He'd have to climb into the car, then out again. Then he would walk through jostling crowds, up and down staircases and finally up the steep steps to the railroad car. To get to his seat, he would have to squeeze past people in narrow corridors and step across the gaps between railcars. At his destination, he would find more staircases and more curbs, another taxicab or private car to enter and exit, and then more stairs at the hotel or church or school where he would give his speech, with people reaching to shake his hand. Finally there would be another set of steps up to the stage.

How could he navigate all that on crutches? Even if he could manage it for a day or two, how could he possibly perform the feat day after day and week after week in a hard campaign?

And once he reached the stage, there he would be, *on crutches*. Just to be seen standing with crutches was to shout to the world, *There's something wrong with me!*

So why not make the campaign in a wheelchair?

By the late twentieth century, sophisticated wheelchairs would make it possible—though never easy—for someone with a disability like FDR's to do one's job and get on with life. This would include politicians. In 1996, the state of Georgia would elect to the U.S. Senate a man named Max Cleland, whose legs and part of one arm had been amputated after a severe injury in the war in Vietnam. He used a wheelchair. In 2014, the people of Texas would elect Greg Abbott as their governor, though Abbott's back had been broken in an accident twenty years earlier and he had relied on a wheelchair ever since.

But in the 1920s, wheelchairs were big, clumsy contraptions seldom seen outside hospitals. More important, city landscapes and buildings had none of the accommodations for wheelchairs that we have now, such as ramps from streets to sidewalks and from sidewalks to building entrances, broad elevators in multistory buildings, and doorways wide enough for wheelchairs.

Besides, anyone in a wheelchair was assumed to be incapable of an active life. FDR must have held a memory of the ungainly wheelchair that his grandfather, Warren Delano Jr., once a vigorous and powerful man, was forced to use at the end of his life. It was hardly the image of a person who could lead and command others.

For use at home, FDR had a couple of narrow kitchen chairs converted to wheelchairs so that servants, nurses, and family members could push him easily from one room to another.

But campaigning in a wheelchair, not to mention holding an important position in government, was unthinkable.

So reliance on a wheelchair was out, and crutches were hardly any better.

To reach his goal, FDR simply had to find some new treatment, some new exercise, some way of transforming his condition so that he might finally bring his legs back to life.

He talked it over with Dr. Lovett. He knew the orthopedist had no miracle medicines to offer. Still, there had to be *something* else he could do.

Well, Lovett said, some of his patients had made commendable progress by exercising in tanks of water, even in the Atlantic Ocean.

The foundation of Lovett's whole approach to helping polio patients was exercise. But as FDR knew by now, working out with damaged muscles led quickly to exhaustion. Even a determined patient couldn't keep it up for long. So improvement over time was agonizingly slow. But water helps to support one's weight, making it easier to exercise for long periods.

The logic struck FDR immediately, and he decided to try it out.

Chapter 7

"I AM INTERESTED IN TOO MANY THINGS"

Deep in FDR's memory, well-being was linked to water.

In 1890, when Franklin was eight years old, his father had suffered a heart attack at the age of sixty-three. To recover his health, James Roosevelt crossed the Atlantic with his wife and son to visit a town in Germany called Bad Nauheim. Here, people with heart trouble and other ailments soaked in warm pools fed by mineral-rich springs that foamed out of the earth. Many people of the late 1800s, including a number of doctors, believed the bubbling waters brought benefits to people with heart trouble. Maybe they did, or maybe they didn't—even then many other doctors doubted it—but it was certainly soothing to soak in the warm, salty pools. The treatment went on day after day, often for several weeks. The Roosevelts returned to Bad Nauheim for several summers, and they believed the mineral waters did James a great deal of good, since he lived for ten more years.

So when Dr. Lovett recommended exercising in water, FDR's enthusiasm may have drawn upon those pleasant memories of his father's experience with the "water cure" in Germany.

When the spring weather of 1922 turned warm enough, FDR asked the men who worked on the Roosevelt estate to lower him into a narrow pond where a dam blocked the creek that ran through the woods. He had splashed and swum there as a boy. Now, as long as he could stand the cold, he could enjoy the benefits of exercising in water not far from his back door.

And he had another idea. A friend of his, Vincent Astor, one of the richest men in America, owned an estate in Rhinebeck, New York, just fifteen miles up the Hudson from Hyde Park. One of its remarkable features was an indoor swimming pool, perhaps the first of its kind in a private residence in the United States. When FDR told Astor about Dr. Lovett's suggestion, Astor invited him to drive up and use the pool, which Roosevelt found to be even better for his exercises than the pond, since the water was warmer. "The legs work wonderfully in the water," he told Dr. Draper, "and I need nothing to keep myself afloat."

"All is going well," he wrote a friend in July, "and I am getting more muscular control every day."

"Swimming is our great sport," he wrote to one of Eleanor's aunts, "either in Vincent Astor's tank or our own pond!"

One day at the pond, a man who worked for the Roosevelts, Louis DePew, heard FDR call out: "Well, the water got me where I am, and the water has to bring me back!"

Now, what did he mean by *that*?

Was he thinking of Bear Mountain, where the poliovirus may have tainted the lakes at the Boy Scout camp?

That's possible. There's no record of FDR saying he believed he'd picked up the virus from the water at Bear Mountain. Then again, as a leader of the Boy Scouts, he might have kept any such suspicion to himself.

Or was he blaming his accidental dunking in the Bay of Fundy, where the water had felt "so cold it seemed paralyzing"? That's unlikely, since he knew that polio was caused by an infectious virus, not by immersion in cold water.

Either way, that stray remark reveals that when FDR's mind wandered to the origins of his paralysis, he thought of water. Then, it seems, he drew an imaginary line between the water that had carried the virus and the water here in his own pond. And for just that moment, he conceived a little game of magical make-believe: In the summer of 1921, water had left him paralyzed. Now, a year later, he imagined that he might be immersed in water and come back out on the strength of his own legs.

———————•◆•———————

As the fall of 1922 gave way to winter, the Roosevelts were back in New York City, where there was no place for FDR to continue his water exercises. Soon he went to Eleanor with a new idea.

He was thinking, he told her, of renting a houseboat for a long cruise through the Florida Keys, the string of low, semitropical islands that stretch for 120 miles into the Caribbean Sea. He could invite a few friends along and try some fishing, and he could get into the warm waters of the Caribbean for more exercise. What did she think? Would she come along?

She hesitated. She had the children to manage. She didn't like vacations in the wintertime. And she wasn't sure they should spend the money. (For six weeks of cruising, the cost of a boat and crew would be about $1,500—no small expense even for the well-off Roosevelts.)

"Well," he said, "I think I might as well do as much as possible in order to improve as much as I can, because I shouldn't be any greater burden than is necessary."

Eleanor later said this was the only time she ever heard him speak so bluntly about the trouble his condition caused his family. It reminded her "that much of his gallant joking was merely a way of forcing himself to accept cheerfully what he could not help."

For that reason, or simply because her husband wanted so much to take this trip, she said yes.

———— ◆ ————

He found a comfortable houseboat to rent called *Weona II*, fifty-eight feet from bow to stern, with two decks and a motorboat for fishing. Carrying FDR, a small crew, a few friends, Missy LeHand, and Eleanor (who came along for just the first few days), the vessel sailed out of Miami in mid-February 1923, then turned southwest toward the Keys. Soon broad-winged herons and frigate birds were passing overhead. The sun washed over the passengers. The pace was slow and easy.

The deck of a boat presented FDR with entirely new problems in moving around. Two strong men could carry him aboard, but then he had to navigate *Weona*'s narrow passageways and steep staircases on his own. The passageways were too narrow for him to be carried. His wheelchair would be impractical.

But somehow he managed.

He discovered he could take the narrow stairs between decks just as he did at home seated on the stairs and hauling himself up and backward. He told Dr. Lovett that he maneuvered through narrow passageways "by reaching up to the deck beams above, this gave me enough balance and support to move the legs forward in walking." (If he meant that he did that regularly, the claim is hard to credit, given the difficulty of standing with braces on a moving boat. Perhaps he managed it once as an experiment. He may have stretched the facts to impress Lovett.)

Of course the point of the trip was the warm ocean water. But how to get in and out? The deck was ten feet above the waves, and he couldn't just jump in.

He studied the boat's architecture and equipment, then rigged a solution. He described it later in a letter to Dr. Lovett:

> On the top deck where we sat most of the time I
> had a section of the side rail cut out and hinged.
> The forward davit [a small crane for hoisting
> heavy objects] swung around to a position just
> off this opening. From this davit I suspended a
> plain board, like the board of a swing. I then
> sat on the deck, put my feet through the swing,
> pulled it under me. The davit was then swung out
> and I was lowered into the motor boat or, in going
> in swimming, into the water. It was perfectly
> simple once in the water to slide out of the swing
> and to get back into it.

It was an ingenious solution, and FDR was delighted with himself for thinking of it. But then a new obstacle arose, one that he might have anticipated. The waters around the Keys are home to up to a dozen species of sharks. Typically the sharks keep their distance from humans, but even so, *Weona*'s crew apparently advised the passengers not to spend as much time in the water as FDR had been planning.

With that, some people might have concluded that the whole trip was a waste. But FDR just turned his attention to things he could do while safely above the water's surface.

On the deck of the *Weona* were low, comfortable rocking chairs without armrests. They were designed for lazy lounging on sunny afternoons, but FDR now saw them as devices to exercise his legs. At first he had to fight the temptation to rock the chair by the motions of his head and upper body. But with concentration and practice, he told Dr. Lovett, "within a few days I could rock back and forth by using only the knee and the lower leg and foot muscles."

That was calm, quiet work, but he wanted adventure, too. Using his make-shift swing, he had himself lowered into the motorboat. Then he and his friends sped across the blue water for some deep-sea fishing. The big fish they were going after can be brought up only with heavy-duty tackle, and you have to be strapped into special chairs to haul up the heavy lines. When they reached a good place to drop their lines, FDR got himself ready. "At first I tied a strap round my chest and around the back of the revolving fishing chair," he wrote. "This gave the necessary purchase. [He meant that the strap would hold him tight to the chair so that he could exert his strength on the fishing line.] After a little practice I . . . was able to hold heavy fish on a large rod without much difficulty." He reeled in one big fish after another, some weighing forty pounds—not bad for a man who couldn't walk. He must have felt a quiet thrill in discovering that he still could perform difficult feats of coordination and strength.

He was having a ball and getting plenty of exercise, if not quite the type he had planned. And he thought there was another good force at work. He wrote about it later to another man with polio. "I have . . . found for myself one interesting fact which I believe to be a real discovery," he said, "and that is that my muscles have improved with greater rapidity when I could give them sunlight." On his Florida cruise, he said, he had been "much in the open air under the direct rays of the sun with very few clothes on, and there is no doubt that the leg muscles responded more quickly at that time than when I am at home [and] more in the house."

He didn't tell Dr. Lovett about his sunlight theory. The orthopedist probably would have thought it was silly. But now sunlight, like water, was giving FDR another reason to hope for a breakthrough.

Later on, as medical scientists learned more, they would discredit the idea that sunlight could have any good effects on nerves and muscles damaged by polio.

But what science-minded doctors like Dr. Lovett sometimes overlooked was the powerful effect of hope on the mind of a desperate patient.

Dr. Draper, on the other hand, respected what he called "the imponderables" in a patient's recovery. He believed that disease was more complicated than simple infection by a germ; it was a "quarrel" between the germ and its human host, a relationship between "the seed and the soil," as doctors of his school of thought put it. In that quarrel, Draper believed, the patient's mind played its own mysterious role. Dr. Lovett, as an orthopedist, focused on the physical structures of bones and muscles. Dr. Draper considered *everything* that made up the life of a particular patient—not just the parts of his body that could be seen and touched but the traits he had inherited from his ancestors, his emotional and psychological makeup, the environment he lived in, and the complex interactions among all these factors. In the face of that complexity, who could say for sure that regular exposure to sunlight was not helping Franklin Roosevelt—if Roosevelt had developed a powerful belief that it did?

———— ◆ ————

Nurse Lake could hardly believe her eyes. After his time in Florida, her patient now could "set" his right knee, meaning he could hold it firmly in the unbent position. This was a big advance toward the goal of walking by himself. And with only a bit of help, he could sit up from a lying-down position. Perhaps because of his rocking-chair exercises, he had gained power in his quadriceps, the packs of muscle in the front of the thighs. And he could move his feet better than he had before his trip.

"He came back immensely improved from his trip south," Mrs. Lake told Dr. Lovett. He was "looking at least ten years younger."

But then, even more quickly than he had improved, he declined again.

He was feeling so confident that he neglected his exercises, took on a pile of new projects, and stayed up late night after night. Within two weeks of his return, he caught a severe cold and "looked a perfect wreck," according to Nurse Lake. She all but ordered him to Hyde Park for ten days of solid rest. But once he got there, she told Dr. Lovett, he "sat out in the damp" and steadily lost the power he had gained in his quadriceps. Soon he could no longer set his knee or move his feet as he had just a few weeks earlier.

In her private letters to Dr. Lovett, Nurse Lake blamed Eleanor for FDR's setback. Mrs. Roosevelt was always urging Franklin to do this or that during the day, the nurse reported, and then bringing in guests for dinner. The guests would stay too late, FDR would get too little sleep, and the next day he would be exhausted. Mrs. Lake insisted that FDR could make progress only if he kept a single-minded focus on the proper care of his body.

But Eleanor had good reasons for inviting people to dinner so often. She knew her husband's limbs needed exercise, but his brain needed exercise, too. She knew how he loved to keep up with news of what was happening inside the political parties, how he loved to discuss ideas for new policies and laws, how he savored gossip about politicians and friends.

She had never fully shared her husband's confidence that he could learn to walk again and then run for office. (In October 1922, Dr. Draper had written to Dr. Lovett: "His wife told me on the side that she did not feel very sanguine [hopeful].") Now, as the months passed, she was losing whatever hope she might have had.

But even if he never walked again, she believed he must stay active in the affairs of his state and his country.

"I want to keep him interested in politics," she wrote to a friend. "This is what he cares for more than anything else. I don't want him forgotten."

Besides, it really wasn't Eleanor who was distracting FDR from his exercises. He was distracting himself.

About this time he offered some advice to a friend who hoped to make his living as a writer. FDR sent his best wishes but said he doubted the friend could handle such a quiet and lonely life for long. "I can't help feeling that you are built a bit like me," he said, "that you need something physically more active, with constant contact with all sorts of people in many kinds of places." As he told a reporter, "I have never specialized in any one thing. I am interested in too many things."

It was true. When he was supposed to be concentrating on his workouts, he was giving his time to a dozen other pastimes, hobbies, and projects. Some were serious; others, pure fun. He had always been a busy man, but now his hunger to do things seemed insatiable, as if he could defy paralysis just by crowding his days and nights with activity.

For example:

He was a dedicated tree farmer. He directed the planting of thousands of seedlings on the Roosevelts' lands around Hyde Park.

He invested in business ventures.

He designed and built big model sailboats for time trials on the Hudson River.

He made a study of the historic Dutch American farmhouses that lined the valley of the Hudson.

He continued to act as chairman of the regional Boy Scouts organization.

He sent Louis Howe to search shops in New York and Boston for valuable old stamps, books, and art prints, especially pictures of ships and boats. With magnifying glass and tweezers in hand, he sat for hours with his stamps, sorting and studying them for the tales they told of distant places and ages past. He thought everyone should collect stamps. Stamp collecting, he wrote, "dispels boredom, enlarges our vision, broadens our knowledge of geography and in innumerable ways enriches life and adds to its joy."

He started to write a history of the United States. He dropped it after just fourteen pages. "But I had a real idea," he told a friend later. "I thought all our histories lacked movement and a sense of direction. The nation was clearly going somewhere right from the first. I thought I could do better with those ideas than had been done before."

He sent streams of letters to all parts of the country, keeping in touch with Democrats, college friends, navy friends, aunts, uncles, cousins, and countless others, including other people with polio, trading encouragement and ideas for treatments and exercises.

And he read more than he ever had, especially about the past.

"Roosevelt was a walking American history book," Frances Perkins said. "He knew exactly how the troops went here and there . . . He knew exactly what the trading towns were and the trading routes across the valleys." Yet he might also spend half a day reading a book on edible plants.

So his nurses were right. He wasn't doing his exercises as much as he should have, or even as much as he meant to. He was living a full life and stocking his mind with a thousand nuggets of knowledge.

But he was hardly any closer to walking on his own than he had been on the day he first stood up with crutches.

In the spring of 1923, nearly two years since the poliovirus had struck, Dr. Lovett tested the strength of forty-four of FDR's muscles, the same ones he had tested a year earlier. Seven were slightly stronger. Seven were a little weaker. Thirty showed no difference at all.

But month after month, FDR insisted to friends that he was getting better all the time:

APRIL 1923: "My legs are a lot better."

JUNE 1923: "My doctor...is delighted with my
     progress."

JULY 1923: "Though I am still on crutches I hope
     to be able to discard them very soon."

OCTOBER 1923: "A cheerful doctor friend of mine...
     said to me the other day...'You...will get
     better year by year.'"

JANUARY 1924: "The old legs are coming along in good
shape, and I am hopeful that by the end of the
year I can get off at least one crutch and perhaps
a brace."

FEBRUARY 1924: "The legs...are improving
steadily."

He struggled to find something that would make his optimistic predictions come true.

In newspapers and magazines, in letters that came to him from doctors and other polio patients, FDR searched for clues that might lead to a breakthrough treatment. He never fell for the fake doctors and con artists who tried to sell outlandish medical schemes to desperate patients. (He laughed at ads for one "quack medicine" after another. "It may be monkey glands or perhaps it is made out of the dried eyes of the extinct three-toed rhinoceros," he wrote Dr. Draper. "You doctors have sure got imaginations!") But he was open to any experiment or device that seemed to be truly worth a try, whether to strengthen his legs or improve his ability to get around by mechanical means.

He sent for information about a doctor who treated patients by sealing them into a pressurized steel tube as big as a railroad car.

He considered advice about the Whiteley Exerciser, a wall-mounted contraption with rubber cables attached to the patient's legs, and an electric-powered wheelchair that could carry its passenger at a rate of forty miles per hour.

He tried an adult-sized tricycle.

He installed "an old-fashioned children's double-swing" that seemed "to develop the knee muscles in a splendid way."

He studied the designs of Gabriel Bidou, a French doctor who was equipping paralyzed patients with spring-loaded leg braces. "There is no question that the French are far ahead of us in their mechanical appliances," he wrote to a friend with polio. "If you and I do not greatly improve this coming winter [1923–1924] we shall have to get together and work out something along the line of Dr. Bidou's springs."

When he heard about two doctors from Kansas City who were treating their patients with rays from powerful electric lamps, he recalled his experience in the Florida sun and invited the doctors to visit him. Their names were Starr and Barrett. They were osteopaths—doctors who use a system of healing that works more by manipulating patients' body parts than by giving them drugs.

FDR told Starr and Barrett all about his symptoms and the treatments he had tried, then listened closely to what they said. He was impressed, and he wanted to know if their advice was safe. But he knew Dr. Lovett was just about fed up with his enthusiasm for unusual treatments. So he went around Lovett's back.

He wrote to Nurse Lake, saying the letter was just "for your personal and confidential information." He told her the doctors from Kansas City had confirmed his opinion about the good effects of sunlight on damaged nerves. The new doctors had told him "that as I am going at present, the process of muscular development will be very long drawn out, and that the only method of hastening matters is by going to the seat of the trouble—i.e., the nerve cells—and building them up faster than they are building at present. They therefore suggest that I start up here at Hyde Park with a simple light machine . . . i.e., taking an artificial sunbath in my room all over the body for about an hour every morning."

This was "absolutely in line with the undoubted fact which I discovered for myself, that the sun down in Florida, and since I have been up here, has done much to keep the circulation going. For instance, it is absolutely a fact that the mornings I am able to sit in the sun for an hour or two my legs do not get cold in the evening, whereas if the day is cloudy and I do not get my sun bath, the legs freeze up from about 5 p.m. on.

"Don't you (in your purely private and non-professional capacity) agree that it can do no harm to try [the sun-lamp] out at least for a month or two?"

FDR was determined that Dr. Lovett must not know about this new treatment. "I have impressed on Starr the absolute necessity of saying nothing to anybody about the fact that I am taking any treatment from him. I have told him frankly that I do so only as a supplementary experiment and that I have not given up Lovett, do not intend to, and want to be able to discuss the case with Lovett at any time."

FDR used the sunlamp and believed it helped. So, to get more exposure to natural sunlight, he made up his mind to return to Florida for another winter cruise in the early weeks of 1924. This time, instead of renting a boat, he struck a deal with an old friend from college days, John Lawrence, to go in together on the cost of a used houseboat. (Lawrence, too, was recovering from an injury to his legs, though not from polio.) For a new name for the boat, Lawrence suggested they mash up "Lawrence, Roosevelt and Company" to make *Larooco* (pronounced *la-ROW-co*). FDR waded into the agreeable work of equipping the boat, hiring a small crew, planning a schedule, and inviting old friends to come along.

Then, just a few days before he was to board the train for Florida, he had an appointment with Dr. Draper.

The doctor examined his old friend's lower body very carefully. He felt the muscle mass in the thighs and calves. He watched while FDR walked with his braces and crutches.

We do not know exactly what Dr. Draper said to FDR when they sat down to discuss where things stood. But the doctor may have given his patient—as gently and kindly as he could—the same assessment he sent to Dr. Lovett in a letter a few days later.

"I am very much disheartened about his ultimate recovery," Dr. Draper wrote. "I cannot help feeling that he has almost reached the limit of his possibilities."

It had now been two and a half years since the virus had brought him down. For all that time, hard facts had been bombarding his inborn optimism and his fierce determination to recover. Month after month he had shielded himself from these truths. Every time he told a friend that "my legs are a lot better" or that his doctors were amazed by his progress, he was pushing away the plain fact that his legs were hardly better at all and that his doctors were advising him to make the most of what little mobility he had, not to expect a day coming soon when he would rise and walk on his own.

The problem was not what his body could or couldn't do. The real work of a political leader has virtually nothing to do with physical ability. Day by day, a politician's work is to think, to write, and especially to *talk*—to ask questions, discuss possibilities, give instructions, explain a vision, command an audience. Roosevelt could do all those things as well as ever—better, in fact, since polio had given him much more time to read and think things through. Pain and loss had made him wiser, more compassionate. He could understand people as never before. Certainly his gift for talking, whether to a single person or a crowd, was as strong as ever.

No, the problem was not in himself. The problem lay in what others *thought* of him. If they saw only an invalid struck down by a tragic accident, he could never succeed in politics again.

One day shortly before his cruise on the *Larooco*, FDR had welcomed a caller to the house on East Sixty-Fifth Street, a young newspaperman named Lowell Mellett. The two men had never met, and somehow Mellett had never learned of FDR's paralysis. Recalling that day many years later, Mellett told how he had been admitted to the house by Sara Roosevelt's butler, who directed him to the second floor, where visitors were customarily received in the library. Mellett saw FDR waiting at the top of the stairs to greet him, standing straight and holding tight to the heavy railing that crowned the staircase. FDR waved Mellett down the corridor to the library and slowly followed. Mellett looked back, and "I realized then that Roosevelt was propelling himself forward by clasping the railing, hand over hand." Later Mellett went to work for Roosevelt and came to know him well, but "I never got over the hurt of seeing him in his crippled state, either then or afterward."

FDR must have caught the look of shock and regret on Mellett's face—and on the face of everyone as they first met this man who had to go through a pitiable struggle just to walk a few steps in his own house. How could he ever run for office if everyone he met reacted with that expression of pity and fear? In letters to friends he could insist all he wanted that he was getting better by the day, and from a distance they might believe him. But the moment they saw him they would know the truth, just as he must have known it himself in the part of his mind that saw facts as plainly as Lowell Mellett saw them that day by the stairs.

———◆———

Four years earlier, in 1920, he had been his party's rising star. Now, as the election season of 1924 approached, Franklin Roosevelt was in the thoughts of only one important Democrat—Alfred E. Smith, the governor of New York. Smith was preparing for a long-shot campaign to win his party's presidential nomination. And in his view, Roosevelt's physical condition seemed to be not a minus but a plus. A plus for Alfred E. Smith, that is.

The two men, soon to become allies and even friends, were from different worlds.

Al Smith, eight years older than FDR, had grown up roaming the streets of Manhattan's Lower East Side. He came from the sort of working-class Irish, Italian, and German ancestors whom earlier generations of upper-crust Roosevelts had moved uptown to get away from.

Just thirteen when his father died, young Al promptly quit school to earn money cleaning fish and selling newspapers. A smart and friendly kid, he caught the eye of neighborhood politicians, who gave him odd jobs. Soon he was working for Tammany Hall full-time, and when he was only thirty, he was put up for election to the state assembly, and he won. Before long he became the state's most powerful Democrat and a leading voice among the swelling millions of Americans who were first- or second-generation immigrants.

Smith was of the city, Roosevelt of the countryside. Before Smith took his first trip on the New York Central Railroad to the state capital at Albany, he had never seen a farm. He so loved New York that he once said he would rather be a lamppost on Manhattan's Park Avenue than the governor of California. FDR, by contrast, treasured his family's old roots in the rural Hudson Valley, and he liked to call himself a farmer, though his only crop was trees. As an adult, he used New York City as his home base, but he privately called it "this vile burgh" and fled it for tiny Hyde Park whenever he could.

FDR was an Episcopalian, the favored religious denomination of the well-to-do and the powerful. Smith was a proud Catholic, the religion of immigrants who worked in factories and swept the streets.

FDR had learned the law from distinguished professors in wood-paneled rooms at Columbia University. Smith had taught himself the law, sweating over books that he read late at night.

Roosevelt read widely and collected fine books as a hobby. Smith declared he had never read a book for pleasure.

In politics, Smith had become the best-known and most respected product of the Tammany Hall machine. Other Tammany politicians took bribes, but not Al, or so it was said. The Tammany boss "Silent Charlie" Murphy had nurtured Smith's career and steered him clear of trouble, hoping that Al might make Tammany Hall respectable. During Smith's lifetime he was never accused of dirty dealing. But he always bore the brand of the machine.

Smith and FDR differed on the biggest issue of the day—whether to keep or get rid of the unpopular laws known as Prohibition, which, since 1920, had banned the sale of liquor, beer, and wine throughout the United States. Millions of Americans, especially European immigrants with cherished traditions of enjoying wine and beer, wanted Prohibition overturned. Just as fiercely, other millions, especially conservative Protestants in rural America and the South who hated "the demon rum," wanted Prohibition to remain in place.

Like many others, Smith and FDR privately scoffed at Prohibition and drank bootleg beer and liquor in private. (Despite the laws against alcohol, it was still easy to get.) But in public, FDR was a "dry," in favor of enforcing the Prohibition laws. Smith was a "wet," who wanted to do away with them.

In their personal manners the contrast was sharpest of all. One of FDR's favorite expressions from his Harvard days was *infra dig*, short for the Latin phrase *infra dignitatem*, meaning "low class" or "beneath one's dignity." So much about Al Smith, in the eyes of the Roosevelts, was *infra dig*.

Smith chewed on a fat cigar; FDR smoked slim cigarettes in an elegant holder. Smith was legendary for the raspy roar of his voice; Roosevelt spoke in a cultured tenor. Smith played cards with his old pals from the Bowery. FDR, before contracting polio, had golfed and sailed with his old classmates from Harvard.

When Governor Smith was invited to dine at Hyde Park, Sara Roosevelt had to master her emotions to treat him with respect. He was exactly the sort of man who had made her son's entry into politics so appalling to her.

On his side, of course, Smith viewed the Roosevelts as "swells" with barely a clue about what life was really like for most people.

But there was common ground, too.

FDR and Eleanor had long since come to admire Smith's ability to win elections and get laws passed. More than that, like many a progressive New Yorker, they knew the governor truly believed in liberal principles. When a fire killed 146 women workers in New York's Triangle Shirtwaist factory in 1911, Smith was among the leaders who won new laws to make workplaces safer. When conservative clergy argued against a law that would give women and children in the oppressive canning industry one day off a week, Smith stared them down and said: "I have read carefully the commandment 'Remember the Sabbath Day, to keep it holy.' I am unable to find any language in it that says, 'Except in the canneries.'"

Eleanor's respect for Smith had grown during her work for the state Democratic Party. And FDR could not help but like the rollicking governor. "Al Smith could make anybody laugh," a friend said, and FDR was no exception.

Did Smith return FDR's liking and respect? Not so much. The governor saw the younger man as a spoiled upper-cruster just dabbling in politics. And as a proud son of Tammany, Smith resented FDR's history of fighting the organization.

But in 1924, affection was beside the point. Smith was getting ready to run for the Democratic nomination for president, and he perceived that FDR might be able to help him.

Smith's main rival was William Gibbs McAdoo (*MACK-a-doo*), a Californian with strong backing from the party's old rural wing in the West and South. To stand a chance against McAdoo, Smith would need the unified support of his home state's Democrats. Party members in New York City were no problem. They loved Al. But he also needed support upstate, where most people were Protestant, dry, and deeply suspicious of Tammany Hall. The same was true of Protestant Democrats across the country. That's where Roosevelt could help. With his popular last name, his reputation for integrity, and his anti-Tammany record, he could soothe the fears of "the better class of Democrats." If Franklin Roosevelt could support a Catholic "wet" for president, then maybe they could, too.

So Smith asked FDR to be the chairman of his presidential campaign.

If Roosevelt had been able to walk, he might be challenging Smith for the nomination. But now Smith regarded FDR as safely and forever on the political sidelines.

FDR told Al yes, he would be delighted to chair the campaign. Al explained that his staff would do most of the day-to-day work. Roosevelt could hold meetings by phone and in his own home.

This much he could handle. And it would get him back in the game, at least in a small way.

Then Smith made a second request: Would FDR agree to give the main speech nominating Smith for president at the Democratic National Convention? It would be held at New York's biggest arena, Madison Square Garden, in July. Thousands of Democrats from all over the country would be watching his every move and listening to his every word.

That was an entirely different matter.

Chapter 8

"A WILDCAT IN YOUR FACE"

How could he possibly do it?

He had been terribly nervous about showing himself in public. Until recently he had refused even to get in or out of an automobile in daylight. Besides, steps and stairs made it all but impossible to move around in most buildings. Just a few weeks earlier, in January 1924, an old friend from Harvard had written to say he hoped FDR could attend their twentieth class reunion, which would be held in the summer of that year. Very unlikely, FDR replied. "The difficulty lies in the fact that I cannot get up steps with the braces, and therefore have to omit all kinds of functions—that is the only thing that may prevent me from getting on for the 20th anniversary. Even the Democratic Convention in New York will not keep me away as I could not attend the Convention anyway."

Well, could he or not? To do so would mean taking an enormous risk.

He knew Madison Square Garden. He could picture the obstacles it presented to a man in his condition. First, there was the curb between the street and the sidewalk, then the stone step up to the outer doors, then the slippery tile floor in the big lobby. Beyond that were corridors that would be crowded with hurrying people, then the giant arena itself, with its long distances across the floor, and at the end of that trek, steep staircases to the raised platform where he would have to give the speech. And it wasn't just the speech he had to worry about. It was days and nights of acting as Al Smith's floor leader, the person who would have to meet hour after hour with Democratic delegates in closed rooms with armless chairs, or impromptu clutches in the aisles. Every other minute he would face a new chance of crashing to the floor. Of course, he could avoid all that by using a wheelchair, but that would only confirm the suspicion he was determined to quash—that he was still an invalid.

FDR had practiced walking with crutches often enough that he could make it across a room on his own power. But he had to keep LeRoy Jones or Eleanor or one of the boys right by his side, ready to steady him if he started to lose his balance.

What if that happened when he set off across the stage at Madison Square Garden? Every person in that huge arena would remember it forever, including all the reporters.

All that was on one side of his calculations. On the other was the great opportunity that Al Smith had handed him. As Frances Perkins put it, "Everybody had thought he was near to dead." This was his chance to prove he was not only very much alive but still a man ready to play a role on the national scene, still a man to reckon with, perhaps even a man who, if only he might walk someday, still had a future in big-time politics.

How could he give that up? He had to say yes to Smith.

So he did.

But he would have to get ready.

He wanted to show he could walk on his own—with crutches, yes; that was unavoidable—but by himself.

He could not climb the stairs from the convention floor to the speaker's platform by himself. He would have to be carried. No way around that, either.

Then: What would be the setup on the speaker's platform, and how far would he have to walk? The answer, he learned, was about fifteen feet, the length of a large living room. That was the distance between the top of the stairs to the lectern where he would stand for the speech.

FDR chose his oldest son, Jimmy, to be his assistant. Jimmy was sixteen now, tall for his age and strong enough to do the job. It would be a nice touch for the convention delegates to see Roosevelt's son by his side.

In the library of the Roosevelts' townhouse, the boys moved furniture and measured off fifteen feet. Then FDR began to practice the distance with his crutches. From the door to the window, from the window to the door, back and forth he went, making sure with each step not to set either crutch too far in front or too far to the side, until he was too tired and sweaty to do it any longer.

Then again the next day. And the next.

———————◆———————

It was not yet noon on June 27, 1924, but the cavernous hall of Madison Square Garden was already roasting. Ringling Bros. and Barnum & Bailey's Circus had just departed, so the powerful odors of elephants and lions still hung heavy in the damp air. FDR and Jimmy had arrived early, bringing the wheelchair so that FDR could move around and talk with the Democratic delegates gathering on the vast floor of the arena. Up in the galleries, thousands of raucous New Yorkers were starting to yell for their hero, Al Smith. Jimmy could see the beads of sweat rolling down his father's neck.

With many people still milling in the aisles, few noticed when two strong men lifted Roosevelt off his feet and hustled him up the steps to the broad speaker's platform where party leaders were standing, talking, finding their own chairs. Using crutches, with Jimmy standing by, FDR got to his seat.

That was no simple thing, of course, not with the braces that held his legs rigid under his trousers. In a quick series of moves he had performed many times, he pivoted to turn his back to his chair. Then he and Jimmy gripped each other by the arms. Slowly they lowered FDR until he was sitting with his legs locked straight in front of him. Then he reached behind his knees, undid the locks on the braces and pulled his knees up.

The man seated next to him was Joseph Guffey of Pennsylvania, an oil company executive who, like FDR, had been a loyal backer of Woodrow Wilson.

FDR put a hand to Guffey's ear and whispered: "Joe, go up to the pulpit and shake it, will you?"

Guffey gave him a puzzled look. "Why?"

FDR said, "I want to see if it will surely support my weight."

Guffey got it. He went over to the lectern and gave it a hard nudge. It was heavy. FDR could lean against it without pushing it over.

Finally his name was announced. The crowd settled.

Jimmy and his dad now repeated their act in reverse—legs straight, braces locked at the knees, a quick lift and FDR was standing.

Four years earlier, at the Democrats' national convention in San Francisco, many of these same delegates had seen Franklin Roosevelt for the first time. He had been a tall, striking young man of thirty-eight who had seized the big banner of the New York delegation and run to the front of the hall, leading a show of support for the retiring President Wilson, who'd been weakened by a stroke.

Now here he was before them again, the same Franklin Roosevelt, yet different. His legs looked flimsy and unnaturally stiff under his trousers. They saw him grasp his crutches and begin to move. With each step, he carefully placed the crutches in front of him, then pulled his legs along. "Everybody was holding their breath," Frances Perkins said. "The old-line politicians remembered him as a very vigorous young man at the previous convention. Here was this terribly crippled person . . . getting himself to the platform somehow, looking so pale, so thin, so delicate."

One step . . . two steps . . . three steps . . .

He did not fall.

. . . six steps . . . seven . . .

He let go of his left crutch and seized the edge of the lectern. With his right he held down the pages of his speech.

Normally, a politician would toss up his hands and wave to the crowd. But if Roosevelt tried that now, he would crash to the floor.

So instead he tossed up his head—the old gesture that Frances Perkins remembered—and smiled a great, wide smile.

The crowd exploded.

"It just tore the place to pieces," Perkins said.

When the long roar finally faded, FDR began to speak.

It was the same strong voice they remembered—a cultured East Coast voice. He told the vast crowd that ordinary New Yorkers adored Al Smith.

"Ask anyone when you leave this session—ask the woman who serves you in the shop, the banker who cashes your check, the man who runs your elevator, the clerk in your hotel . . ."

Perkins, seated nearby, was watching FDR closely. Even as his voice rang through the hall, she could see his body trembling. The hand holding the pages of his speech on top of the lectern "was literally shaking because of the extreme pain and tenseness with which he held himself up to make that speech," she said.

". . . first in the affections of the people of this state . . . is the man who has twice been honored with election to the governorship . . ."

He scorned the people who had been whispering that Smith, as a Catholic, could not be a loyal American. He called on his party "to be true to ourselves and put from our hearts and minds every sordid consideration, every ignoble personal prejudice."

He said Smith fought for the good of common people. He said no other Democrat was more feared by Republicans.

"He is the happy warrior of the political battlefield . . . this man of destiny whom our state proudly dedicates to the nation—our own Alfred . . . E. . . . Smith!"

Watching from the press gallery was the famous Will Rogers, a comedian, columnist, and actor whose funny writings on public affairs were read all over the country. When FDR called out Smith's name, Rogers wrote, "you would have thought somebody had thrown a wildcat in your face. The galleries went wild."

The enormous crowd whistled and roared for a full hour—for Al Smith, yes, but also for the electrifying performance given by the man who had returned from the edge of the grave.

When Governor Smith had finished his own speech, more people wanted to talk to Roosevelt than to the governor himself. Some were whispering that it ought to be Roosevelt getting the nomination for president, not Smith. "Hell, it's not legs we want in the White House," said one delegate. "It's brains!"

That evening, as FDR rested back at the house on East Sixty-Fifth Street, he heard one of the family's closest friends, Marion Dickerman, come in through the front door downstairs. He called for her to come and see him. He threw his arms up and cried, "Marion . . . I did it!"

———————◆———————

Over the next few days, the newspapers were full of admiring descriptions of FDR's appearance in the Garden. Few reporters took the tone of the writer from the Republican-owned *Los Angeles Times* who sneered at FDR as "hopelessly an invalid . . . obliged to prop himself against the speaker's desk once he had been lifted to his feet." The correspondent from the *Courier-Journal* of Louisville, Kentucky, was much more typical: "There was nothing at the Democratic Convention more inspiring than the heroism of Franklin D. Roosevelt." It wasn't so much Al Smith as his "nominator that loomed large in the picture, an invalid on crutches, perhaps in pain, who conquered the frailties of body by sheer power of will . . . The world abhors the quitter who in his full strength goes down and will not get up. It admires the man who fights to the last . . . Franklin D. Roosevelt showed that this was the stuff he was made of."

The convention soon snarled into a deadlock between the angry forces of Smith and McAdoo, with neither candidate winning enough delegates to be nominated. Every day the July sun pushed temperatures inside the Garden a bit higher, baking the delegates and stretching their nerves. Somehow the deadlock had to be broken. Some new candidate must emerge to unite the party. But the only name mentioned with any enthusiasm was that of Roosevelt, disabled or not. By the second week, another reporter said, that name "would stampede the convention were he put in nomination . . . He has done for himself what he could not do for his candidate."

Delegates asked him, pleaded with him. He said no again and again. At one point a smooth-talking, snappily dressed state senator from New York City, Jimmy Walker, soon to be elected mayor, dropped into the chair next to FDR's and said, "Frank, you are the only man who can be nominated now with any hope." If either Smith or MacAdoo became the nominee, Walker said, half the party would revolt and sit out the election. Only FDR could hold the warring halves together.

FDR didn't even pause to think about it.

"I appreciate the compliment, Jimmy, but it's impossible," he replied. "In the first place, there is my physical condition to consider. And the Smith followers might misunderstand. I'm going to stay with him until the end."

He had only one miracle to perform that summer, and he had pulled it off. He had proven to himself and everyone else that he could cross a stage and give a speech. But he could not possibly run for president—not that year.

Finally, after sixteen days, the exhausted conventioneers turned away from the leaders of their divided party and picked an all-but-unknown lawyer from West Virginia, John W. Davis, as their nominee. FDR and every other savvy

Democrat went home knowing that "Silent Cal" Coolidge, the Republican who had become president a year earlier when Warren G. Harding died in office, was about to win his own four years in the White House.

The convention hadn't even ended before politicians were sitting down with FDR for quiet conversations, asking how soon he could run for some high office.

First in line was Al Smith himself.

Smith had put up a stronger fight for the nomination than many had expected, and already he was planning for another campaign four years hence. He was thinking he might leave the governorship when his term was up at the end of 1924, take a job in private business, save some money, and get ready to run for president again. But he wanted to maintain his power base in New York. For that he needed someone he could control in the governor's chair. Who better than this suddenly popular cripple with the great name?

Again FDR said no. "They have been after me to run for the Governorship in this state," he confided to a friend, "but I have told them that the crutches must go before I run even for dog-catcher."

Still, after three lonely years of being pitied and all but forgotten, it was delightful to have people "after him."

Encouragement was coming from all over the country.

"I have the utmost confidence in you," an Oregon delegate wrote to FDR after the convention, "and would be glad to support you again, if you will get right."

"Like the overwhelming majority of the delegates who attended the convention, I became a very ardent admirer of yours," wrote an Oklahoman, "and had your physical condition permitted, you would have been nominated."

Even the most powerful Democrat in the Midwest, "Boss" Tom Pendergast of Kansas City, had become a fan.

"You know I am seldom carried away," Pendergast wrote to one of his allies in the party, ". . . but I want to tell you that had Mr. Roosevelt . . . been physically able to have withstood the campaign, he would have been named by acclamation the first few days of the Convention. He has the most magnetic personality of any individual I have ever met, and I predict he will be the candidate on the Democratic ticket in 1928."

All these private conversations, all the talk in the papers about how Roosevelt could have had the nomination if only he had wanted it . . . It was a new day.

He had another chance.

But his basic problem was the same as ever.

For many months he had been impatient with Dr. Lovett's cautious, one-step-at-a-time approach to his treatment.

FDR went to Lovett and said he must find some new way of recovering strength in his legs. What more could be done?

Lovett hardly knew what to say. Three years had gone by since the virus had attacked FDR. The nerves it destroyed were never coming back to life. Roosevelt's one chance for improvement lay in the exercises Lovett had already prescribed. With a little more strength and more practice, he could get better and better with his canes and crutches. That was about it.

The two men were deadlocked.

FDR decided he had learned all he could from Lovett. If he couldn't find a doctor with new advice, he would have to be his own doctor.

PART 3

GETTING READY

· ·

FALL 1924– SUMMER 1928

Chapter 9

SOMETHING IN THE WATER

One day during the endless infighting at the Democratic convention in 1924, FDR fell into conversation with a friend from his Washington days, a wealthy banker named George Foster Peabody. When Roosevelt mentioned that he was looking for new ways to restore life to his legs, Peabody told him a story.

Some years earlier, Peabody had helped fix up the old resort of Saratoga Springs in upstate New York. It was a spa with mineral springs, like the ones in Germany that FDR had visited as a boy with his mother and father. Soaking in the Saratoga waters, Peabody had thought back to a much smaller resort in rural Georgia, his home state, that he had visited often as a boy. When he went south to see what had become of the old place—it was called the Meriwether Inn—he found it worn and all but deserted. But the water was the same as ever, gushing up from the depths of nearby Pine Mountain at a steady temperature of 89 degrees, suffused with minerals that made the water fizzy with tiny bubbles. It flowed into a broad outdoor swimming pool.

For as long as anyone could remember, people had been attracted to the spot by the water's restorative powers. First it had been Muscogee (Creek) people who said the water healed their wounds, then American tourists who made the place a popular resort for the well-to-do in the late 1800s. The nearby village was called Bullochville, otherwise known in the region as Warm Springs.

Peabody thought the resort might be brought back to its former stature and success, like Saratoga Springs. So he bought the rights to purchase the place, thinking he could pass it along to a new owner who would devote full time to it—perhaps the state of Georgia itself. In the meantime he worked with the man who had been running it, a retired and sickly newspaper editor named Tom Loyless.

It was Loyless who told Peabody the remarkable story that Peabody now relayed to Franklin Roosevelt. It was about what had happened to a young man with polio who ventured into the swimming pool.

His name was Louis Joseph. He was an engineer in his twenties. While working in the West Indies, he had caught the poliovirus and lost the use of his legs. He had to quit his job and moved back to his parents' home in Columbus, Georgia, the city nearest to Bullochville. For a vacation in 1921, the family spent some time at the Meriwether Inn. Every day, Louis got into the swimming pool and moved around. He came back the next summer and the next.

After three summers of exercise in the foamy water, Louis Joseph could walk with a cane.

FDR listened, interested but not terribly impressed. He had heard many tales of miraculous treatments for polio, and he knew that most were exaggerations, if not pure hype.

But Peabody wasn't through. When the Democratic convention was over, he wrote letters to Louis Joseph and Tom Loyless, asking them to send detailed accounts of Louis's recovery.

FDR now read these words in Louis Joseph's letter:

> I was almost completely paralyzed with the exception of my arms. Discovering that I could swim in the warm water here, after someone helped me into the pool, I returned. This is my third summer. I use a cane while walking in the street, and can get about well.

A third-hand story had been one thing. But here in this letter was an amazing testament written by hand in Louis Joseph's own words.

FDR already knew that water made it easier for him to exercise. What if the natural minerals in the warm Georgia water could do something more?

A new plan bloomed in his mind. To a New York doctor who had built him some new leg braces he wrote: "I am planning to go to Warm Springs, Georgia on October 3rd to try out a remarkable swimming pool of natural highly mineralized water . . . I have had such success with sunlight and swimming that I believe that in such a pool I could actually walk around at the shallow end with the water up to my shoulders, and thereby get the normal walking motion better than any other way. I can stand up without support in water just below my shoulders and I am going to take a couple of canes into the pool with me . . .

"There is nothing like trying it out."

He rearranged his business affairs to guarantee the time he would need. Van Lear Black would tolerate his long absences indefinitely, but he had to quit his law firm, where his partners were about out of patience. He formed a new firm with a very bright young lawyer he had met, Basil O'Connor—and this time Roosevelt's name came first on the door.

Then he packed his bags.

Franklin, Eleanor, Missy LeHand, and LeRoy Jones arrived at the Warm Springs train station in early October 1924. The scent of pine woods and a view of soft green hills greeted them. By an odd coincidence, the village, population 470, had originally been named for the family of Eleanor's grandmother, a southern belle named Mittie Bulloch Roosevelt. But neither Franklin nor Eleanor had ever been near the place. Even for the rural South, it was isolated. In the day's fading light, the Roosevelts caught glimpses of a broken-down hotel with peeling paint, a collection of sagging white cottages, and a slumping dance pavilion. Eleanor thought the whole place was depressing. But FDR insisted it was "delightful and very comfortable."

The next morning, he was eager to get straight to the swimming pool. But first he opened the door to welcome Louis Joseph himself, standing and walking with only the help of a cane. With him was a local doctor named James Johnson, who had witnessed Louis's progress. Roosevelt questioned them closely. They said the water held no miracles. It would take time to see any improvement. But the water made it easy to exercise. There was no doubt about that.

FDR got into his swimming trunks. With LeRoy Jones at his side, he made his way to the pool's edge. An artificial waterfall spilled into the pool at one end. The water reflected the painted ocean-blue of the concrete sides. Soft white sand lay across the bottom.

Grasping a cane in either hand, he slipped in.

At home in New York, unless he was sitting in direct sunlight or a hot bath, his legs were always cold.

But now he felt a delicious warmth seep up through his feet into his calves, thighs, and abdomen. The sparkling sensation of a million carbonated bubbles ran up and down his skin, as if he had plunged into a pool of warm ginger ale.

His arms and hands bobbed upward as if propelled by hands below the surface. He had the sudden sense of shedding twenty or thirty pounds.

A chemist might have told him the minerals made the water denser than ordinary water, so anything floating in the pool at Warm Springs would rise higher and faster than it would in ordinary water. But whatever the chemistry, the sensations were akin to magic.

Squeezing the handles of his canes, FDR eased away from Roy. Then he was standing alone on his own two feet. He began to move around. After three years of struggling to accomplish his exercise routine, this seemed so amazingly easy.

He shouted, "I don't think I will ever get out!"

Day after day through the rest of October 1924, he became more convinced that, as he wrote to a disabled friend back in New York, "it is a really remarkable cure. The swimming pool is splendid and I walk around in water 4 [feet] deep without braces or crutches almost as well as if I had nothing the matter with my legs."

Riding in Tom Loyless's car, exercising in the pool, sitting on the porch of the Meriwether Inn, he began to imagine what the water at Warm Springs might mean to other people struggling in the aftermath of polio.

Eleanor said that since the diagnosis at Campobello, she had never heard her husband mention golf, the sport he loved most. But now, at Warm Springs, he allowed himself to dream about it. Before long, he wrote an old friend, "I hope . . . I shall try my hand at golf again."

To his mother he wrote: "When I get back I am going to have a long talk with Mr. George Foster Peabody . . . I feel that a great 'cure' for infantile paralysis and kindred diseases could well be established here."

He revised his calendar for the coming months—late 1924 and early 1925. After Christmas and New Year's at home, he would return to Florida for two months of cruising the Keys aboard the *Larooco* and exercising in the warm Caribbean. Then, when spring reached central Georgia, he would come back to the water at Warm Springs.

———— ◆ ————

Missy LeHand was proving to be not just an excellent secretary but an all-around assistant. She had learned to read her boss superbly, knew his moods, spotted what he needed before he knew it himself. Shrewd and practical, she had learned which people he wanted to cultivate and which he wanted to avoid. She learned his writing style so well that she could draft many of his letters for him. She worked hard and was utterly dependable and efficient, but she knew how to relax and have fun, too—a skill that Eleanor, for all her remarkable qualities, never learned.

Gradually the professional relationship between boss and secretary turned into an affectionate friendship, then a mutual dependence that would lead many to say that Missy was FDR's "office wife." Was it more than affection? No one ever knew. When Eleanor had learned of her husband's romantic affair during World War I, she had insisted that Franklin break if off. She realized now that FDR, in his long absences from home, enjoyed his "times with Missy." But she treated Missy like a member of the family, even as a daughter, and never suggested that Missy and her husband were inappropriately close.

Quite possibly she realized that Missy, by tending to the details of Franklin's busy life, freed Eleanor to pursue her own increasingly crowded schedule. She was becoming a power in New York politics in her own right, a leading voice for the role of women in the Democratic Party. She cared for her husband's welfare, but she had no desire to trail along in his wake and serve his every need from New York to Florida to Georgia and back again.

What mattered most about Missy LeHand were her sharp intelligence and her cool good judgment. She had come up by her own wits, leaving a working-class Catholic family in Boston to make her own living in Washington and New York. She was one more person, like Louis Howe and Basil O'Connor, who helped FDR see the world through the eyes of people who hadn't grown up on a landed estate and gone to Harvard.

———— ◆ ————

The leaders of the Allies in World War II, meeting at Tehran, Iran, in 1943—Premier Joseph Stalin of the Soviet Union, FDR, and Prime Minister Winston Churchill of the United Kingdom.

The original statue of FDR at the Franklin Delano Roosevelt National Memorial in Washington, D.C., shrouded his disability. After disability advocates said his wheelchair should be plainly displayed, this statue, by the sculptor Robert Graham, was added in 2001. The inscription on the wall, quoting Eleanor Roosevelt, reads: "Franklin's illness . . . gave him strength and courage he had not had before. He had to think out the fundamentals of living and learn the greatest of all lessons—infinite patience and never-ending persistence."

As the economic crisis deepened in 1931-32, homeless people were forced to build makeshift villages of scrap metal and wood. Soon they were known as "Hoovervilles."

A banner on Franklin Street in Worcester, Massachusetts, promotes Roosevelt's first campaign for president.

FDR's thousand-watt smile was a powerful political tool. Here he exhibits it in an outdoor speech during the 1932 presidential campaign.

FDR's victory in the 1928 governor's race had been razor-thin. But in 1930 he won reelection in a landslide, as the next day's *New York Journal* reported. His victory made Roosevelt the leading Democrat in the race to challenge President Herbert Hoover, whose popularity had plummeted in the onset of the Great Depression.

Early in his 1928 campaign for governor of New York, FDR shifted from a railroad car to the back seat of an automobile, where he could greet voters and even give a speech without leaving the car.

Just elected governor, FDR poses with his political ally Al Smith, who soon came to resent FDR's determination to run his own show in the state capital of Albany. (Note the leg braces exposed at FDR's feet—a rejoinder to those who claimed he shielded all signs of his disability from public view.)

Roosevelt was delighted with his design of hand controls for a used Ford. The contraption worked, and from then on, he often drove around his properties in Georgia and Hyde Park—his only means of movement entirely within his own control.

Marguerite LeHand, nicknamed "Missy" by the Roosevelt children, rose from a working-class background to become not only FDR's personal secretary but his close political adviser and friend. "Missy is my conscience," he often said.

FDR developed strength and coordination by endless back-and-forth practice on a long set of planks with handrails. Here he practices at Warm Springs with two other polio survivors, including his friend, the popular Fred Botts, who had trained to be an opera singer.

On a hot day at Warm Springs, a photographer captured FDR fishing alone. He had traded long trousers for shorts, revealing his leg braces.

Roosevelt cried, "I can walk!" then was held up for a photo by his assistant, LeRoy Jones (left), and Dr. William McDonald. (His wheelchair is just behind him.) The doctor had urged FDR to pursue a new exercise program without wearing braces, but the workouts damaged his legs.

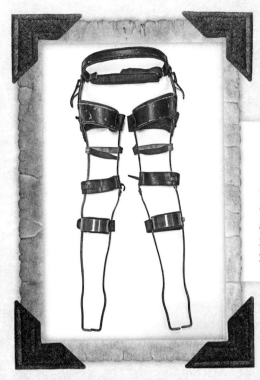

These leg braces were one of several sets made for FDR. Leather straps with buckles at the waist, buttocks, hips, knees, and thighs were attached to frames made of aluminum or steel. Locks at the knees kept the braces rigid when FDR was standing.

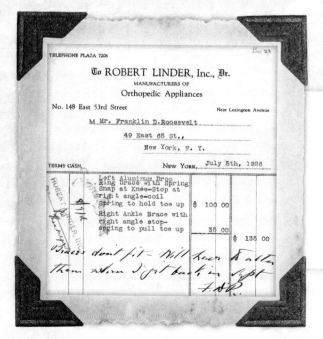

Roosevelt struggled to find braces that suited him but was never satisfied. This receipt includes his note to the maker of a new set: "Braces don't fit. Will have to alter them when I get back in Sept. FDR."

Roosevelt's rave reviews attracted other polio survivors to Warm Springs from across the U.S. Soon he was calling himself "Old Doctor Roosevelt" and directing their exercises.

In the company of others who had been paralyzed, FDR lost his self-consciousness about his atrophied legs.

Roosevelt poses at Warm Springs with two boys on bicycles.

The mineralized water in the Warm Springs pool felt so good that FDR cried: "I don't think I will ever get out!"

Louis Howe, a cantankerous newspaperman turned behind-the-scenes political operative, saw FDR's early promise and stuck with him through his greatest ordeal.

Frances Perkins—the labor advocate who was Roosevelt's friend, aide, and close observer throughout his career—said the core of his character was "a capacity for living and growing that remained to his dying day. It accounts for his rise from a rather unpromising young man to a great man—not merely a President but a man who so impressed himself upon his time that he can never be forgotten."

After the convention, FDR, on crutches, greets
John W. Davis, the Democrats' nominee for president
(center), and New York governor Al Smith (right) at
the Roosevelts' home in Hyde Park.

Before the Democratic National Convention, FDR
practiced for days to be sure he could walk on crutches
to the podium at Madison Square Garden in New York.

His speech nominating
Al Smith for president
electrified the delegates,
resurrecting his own chances
to run for office. But the
enthusiastic response of his
fellow Democrats doubled the
pressure he felt to regain
the ability to walk unaided.

Eleanor Roosevelt sat for this portrait not long before poliomyelitis struck her husband. She was just beginning her own work as an activist in the Democratic Party.

FDR in 1924, the year he reentered the public arena as chair of Al Smith's campaign for president. Even under a suit coat, the expansion of his upper body is evident.

A portrait of the Roosevelt family in 1919. Seated, from left, are Franklin Jr. (on his father's lap), FDR, Eleanor, John (on Eleanor's lap), and James. Standing, from left, are Anna and Elliott.

FDR waves to supporters during his 1920 campaign for vice president. He was a golfer, sailor, and tennis player. Friends recalled that he jogged from one meeting to the next as assistant secretary of the U.S. Navy.

Franklin as a teenager, posing with his father and mother, James and Sara Delano Roosevelt. He was close to both parents, but James, who was 26 years older than his wife, died when FDR was in his first year of college at Harvard.

FDR holds his second-eldest son, Elliott, at Campobello Island around 1912.

As a veteran of the news business, Tom Loyless, the manager of Warm Springs, knew what a single well-placed story could mean to the fortunes of a struggling business. So he got in touch with editors at Georgia's biggest newspaper, the *Atlanta Journal-Constitution.*

He said, *Why not send someone to write up a story about Franklin Roosevelt's quest to recover from infantile paralysis in a forgotten little resort in west Georgia?* It would be a good story for a Georgia paper, especially with FDR back in the public eye after his performance at Madison Square Garden.

So the newspaper sent a young writer named Cleburne Gregory, who spent most of one day chatting and rambling around with FDR. Roosevelt could hardly stop talking about the wonders of the place. Gregory went back to Atlanta captivated by the man's enthusiasm and charm.

He wrote:

"Mr. Roosevelt does not know how he contracted the dread disease . . . All he does know is that he was hit, and hit hard, with the result that both of his legs were immovable for many months. Gradually he acquired the skill necessary to drag himself around on crutches . . .

"The distinguished visitor has the large swimming pool all to himself for two hours or more each day. He swims, dives, uses the swinging rings and horizontal bar over the water, and finally crawls out on the concrete pier for a sun bath that lasts another hour. Then he dresses, has lunch, rests a bit on a delightfully shady porch, and spends the afternoon driving over the surrounding country, in which he is intensely interested . . .

"'I am deriving wonderful benefit from my stay here,' Mr. Roosevelt said. 'This place is great. See that right leg? It's the first time I have been able to move it at all in three years.'

"Mr. Roosevelt does not attribute any medicinal effects to the Warm Springs waters, but he gives the water credit for his ability to remain in it for two hours or more, without tiring in the least, and the rest of the credit for his improvement is given to Georgia's sunshine . . . With him everything in Warm Springs is 'great' or 'fine' or 'wonderful.' That is the spirit that has carried him to remarkable heights for a man just past his fortieth year, and it is the spirit that is going to restore him to his pristine health and vigor."

FDR was happy to help generate a little regional publicity for Warm Springs. He did not know the *Atlanta Journal-Constitution* would sell Cleburne Gregory's feature story to other newspapers. In the next few weeks, the story appeared in big-city dailies and small-town weeklies from New York to California, with headlines like FRANKLIN ROOSEVELT WILL SWIM TO HEALTH, accompanied by photos of a grinning FDR at the edge of the pool at Warm Springs.

Important Democrats spotted the story and read it.

So did people who had polio, desperate people who had spent months and years shut away from the pitying eyes of "normal" people, losing any hope of leading full and happy lives.

And now they were reading the words of the paralyzed Franklin Roosevelt, talking of a return to "pristine health and vigor."

———— ◆ ————

Back aboard his houseboat in January 1925, FDR soon realized he would have to drop his idea of using the Caribbean as an exercise pool. It just wasn't practical—not around the Florida Keys. He enjoyed life aboard the house-boat, but there were simply too many sharks cruising the shallows for him to spend much time in the water.

Then one day in the *Larooco's* launch boat he had an accident. Muscles in his right knee were torn. His leg turned black and blue. Complete rest was essential. He would not be able to exercise again until he got back to Warm Springs—three months of waiting to do anything at all to help his legs. Missy LeHand said there were days aboard the boat when he could not get out of bed and face the day until noon.

It was the worst injury from a fall he had suffered so far, but it was hardly the only time he had fallen. Indeed, one of his main reasons for wanting greater strength and balance was to reduce the danger of falls. They were not only frightening and painful. If he fell hard enough, he could wind up worse off than he was already, not to mention humiliated if a fall occurred in public.

He was always at risk. When standing with his braces, he could easily lean a bit too far to one side and find it impossible to recover his balance. When walking with crutches, he could move one foot just an inch too far, and down he would go. A helper might lose his grip on FDR for a second, and down he would go. The muscles of his lower abdomen, thighs, and buttocks were so weak that if he wasn't careful, he could fall out of a chair.

Basil O'Connor, Roosevelt's new law partner, had seen it happen. In fact, he had seen FDR fall the first time he ever set eyes on him.

One morning O'Connor had arrived for work at his office building in lower Manhattan to find a little group of people watching as a tall man on crutches moved slowly through the front door into the lobby. He was being assisted by another man; O'Connor guessed he was a servant or a chauffeur.

O'Connor recognized the man with crutches as Franklin Roosevelt. He had seen his picture in the newspapers. Now he watched as FDR struggled toward the elevator across the polished stone floor of the lobby. His legs were stiffly straight from his waist to his feet. The chauffeur stood just to his left, watching closely. Roosevelt's progress was slow. Each movement required a series of smaller movements. First he would lean heavily on the crutches. Then he would toss his head back to pull his weight off the crutches for a second. In that instant, he thrust the crutches ahead, aiming the tip of the left crutch (on his weaker side) to a point on the slick floor where the chauffeur had planted his foot to keep the crutch from slipping. Then FDR would lean forward on the crutches and haul his lower body along.

O'Connor could see that the muscles of his neck were tight with the strain.

FDR had gone a short distance when the tip of the left crutch landed with a little too much force against his helper's shoe. Suddenly he was falling.

The chauffeur leaped to catch him, but it was too late. Down FDR crashed, crutches clattering, hat skittering across the floor. The chauffeur tried to pull him up by his armpits, but he was too heavy. Watchers rushed to help.

"Nothing to worry about!" FDR called. O'Connor said his voice sounded "pleasant and strong," with "a ring in it."

Lying on the floor, trying to twist up to a sitting position, FDR looked up at O'Connor and called, "Give me a hand there."

To another man he said the same thing, then: "All right, now, all together!"

In a moment he was up on his crutches again.

He nodded to the chauffeur and said, "Let's go."

Later he was paid a visit at Hyde Park by a distant cousin named Nicholas Roosevelt. FDR suggested a drive around the estate. As Nicholas Roosevelt watched, two helpers carried FDR down the steps from the front door to the waiting auto. They got him into his seat, but "as they turned and left him he lost his balance . . . and he fell over on the car seat. I doubt if one man in a thousand as disabled and dependent on others would have refrained from some sort of reproach, however mild, to those whose carelessness had thus left him in the lurch. But Franklin merely lay on his back, waved his strong arms in the air, and laughed. At once they came back and helped him to his seat . . . and he called me to join him. For a moment I had seen the true spirit of the man. He was not putting on an act. Rather it was the instinctive reaction of a brave and gallant gentleman—as illuminating as it was moving and inspiring."

———————— ♦ ————————

When Roosevelt's injured leg had healed, he returned to Warm Springs—the official new name taken by Bullochville—and got straight to work. With the pool to himself all morning long, he alternated periods of exercise and sunbathing. He had a table placed in the water about a foot below the surface. Here he could sit and make his legs move this way and that. His optimism flowed back.

He had been at the resort for only a couple of days when a message arrived.

A polio survivor had just been helped off the train from Atlanta. She said her name was Thelma Steiger. She was from Missouri. She wanted to know where to find the healing waters.

There was a young man at the station, too—one Lambert Hershheimer, from Falmouth Heights, Massachusetts. He asked the same question.

FDR and Tom Loyless looked at each other. Both had been getting letters from people like this, people who had polio or their parents, who wanted to know: If they came to Warm Springs, could they be cured?

All the letter-writers had read Cleburne Gregory's newspaper story, with its glowing optimism about Warm Springs. Now, with the coming of spring, a few of them, in their search for a cure, had simply boarded trains bound for Georgia. And here they were.

Where would they sleep? FDR was staying in one of the few nice cottages at the resort, lent to him by the owners. But the Meriwether Inn was a falling-down disaster. Most of the resort's cottages had no heat or running water. Even the nicest and biggest was so dilapidated that FDR called the place "the Wreck." And of course there was no staff to see to the special needs of disabled people, let alone to help them get better.

So Roosevelt and Loyless had been writing back to say they were very sorry but they couldn't help—not now, anyway.

But here were these people at the railroad station, with desperate hopes and no place to stay.

FDR and Loyless asked around in the village and found a couple of homeowners who agreed to house the visitors.

The next day's train brought a young man from Pennsylvania who looked more like a scarecrow than a man. He had made the trip in the baggage car, sitting in his wheelchair among three sacks of mail, some chicken crates, and a coffin. His brother had come along to help him.

The man in the wheelchair was named Fred Botts. He had come down with infantile paralysis in the epidemic of 1916 and never taken another step. For nine years he had been cooped up in his parents' house, dwindling to skin and bones. Then his father noticed the story about FDR and Warm Springs in the local newspaper. Botts had once hoped to become an opera singer and still had his lovely baritone voice, so his family arranged for him to perform at their church for friends who donated money to hear him sing, and he used the money to buy train tickets to Georgia. He was so emaciated that FDR thought he looked like he was in the late stages of tuberculosis, often called "consumption" because it seemed to consume the body pound by pound.

Over the next few days more people with arms and legs damaged by "infantile" trickled into town.

FDR was there to work on his own recovery. He had neither the time nor, to be honest, the proper professional training to help these strangers.

But their need, so like his own, spoke to him. Perhaps he could do something for them. After all, he had spent many hours in conversation with the nation's leading experts in after-polio treatments, and he had his own ideas, based on intensive personal experience, about which treatments worked best.

So one by one, he began to quiz the newcomers about their cases, and he sized up the strength left in their limbs.

Some were better off than he—a teenaged girl from Boston who could walk with only one brace, for instance, and a nineteen-year-old boy from Alabama who could walk well with crutches. Some were worse off. Fred Botts, with "practically nothing below the hips," was one of those. Mrs. Steiger from Missouri was in the same boat. FDR thought a man in his thirties named Rogers, from Wisconsin, had hurt his early chances of recovery by returning to work only three weeks after contracting the disease. "He had made up his mind that nothing could ever be done," FDR said, but now Rogers had grasped at one last straw by traveling to Warm Springs.

FDR and Tom Loyless asked a few people from the village to help with pushing wheelchairs and getting people in and out of the pool. They spoke frankly to the visitors. There was no staff of doctors and nurses here, they said. Together, they would all have to be their own doctors. Then they got into the pool, and Franklin Roosevelt began to teach them the exercises he had learned from Kathleen Lake and Wilhelmine Wright.

From the moment Fred Botts was lowered in, he was delighted.

"The water was of the most pleasing temperature," he remembered later, "not so cold that it would chill a person, nor so warm that it would enervate." He had not been able to move by himself in nine years. Now, with inner tubes keeping him upright, "I paddled around with my hands and was surprised with what little ease I could move my legs . . . The gentle caress of the water as we moved our limbs through it had a most stimulating effect." It was as if his legs and arms were all being massaged at once, and he was free of gravity's burden.

In the shallow end, about three feet deep, FDR got himself seated on the bottom with water up to his shoulders for support. One by one he had each "patient" sit on the edge of the pool with legs extended. He would gently grasp one of their legs and begin to move it. "Just hang on," he would say, "and concentrate on kicking while I move your legs." Up and down, up and down— "Move along with me, and before you know it, you'll be moving by yourself— that's the beauty of this water!" In a different spot there was a strong bar for swimmers to grab while moving their legs from side to side—a different motion for different muscles. FDR demonstrated. "Catch hold of the bar this way," he would say. "Now . . . swing . . . in and out . . . Hard! Harder! That's it . . . that's fine! Now, again, this way . . ."

He was soon calling himself "Old Doctor Roosevelt." He began to make charts recording the strength in the patients' muscles so they could keep track of improvements over time. He said they had been sitting still for so long that even their good muscles had gone to sleep. This was the time and place to wake them up, in the sparkling waters of the Warm Springs pool.

Two of the patients, Thelma Steiger and Dorothy Weaver, were women of generous proportions. FDR was determined to help them place their feet on the bottom of the pool and keep them there. "One of these ladies," he recalled later, "had great difficulty in getting both feet down to the bottom of the pool. Well, I would take one large knee and I would force this large knee down, then I would say, 'Have you got it?' and she would say, 'Yes,' and I would say, 'Hold it, hold it.' Then I would reach up and get hold of the other knee very quickly and start to put it down and then number one knee would pop up." This would go on until the three of them were laughing so hard they had to take a break. The next day, and the next, they worked at it again. And by the time he left the resort a few weeks later, he recalled, "I could get both those knees down at the same time."

None of them had ever laughed about polio. Now, with each other, they could laugh all they wanted, because they all knew the strange and funny frustrations of limbs that refused to obey their commands.

After a session of thirty minutes in the pool, FDR would call out, "All right now, everybody stay in the sun for an hour!" FDR would tell them tales about his own effort to recover. "You've got to *know* you're going to improve," one of the visitors remembered him saying. "Keep yourselves mentally alert. Don't lose contact with the things you enjoyed before infantile paralysis." Then—back into the pool for another half hour, followed by a final half hour of sunbathing.

Sometimes in the late afternoon they would gather on the creaking veranda of the inn to sip cool drinks and talk some more. What a luxury— since the disease had struck, who had they spoken to who really understood?

A young girl from the village named Ruth Stevens sometimes came to sit and listen, bringing wild violets for Fred Botts, whom she especially liked.

One day she heard Mr. Roosevelt say, "I hope my medical fraternity will allow me to come back and practice here. I feel I'm rather good at giving exercise in the water."

———————◆———————

Two weeks rolled by, then three and four. In the evenings, FDR invited guests for steak dinners. In the afternoons he took motor jaunts with Loyless to see the countryside around Warm Springs. They stopped to chat with farmers about crops and with politicians about campaigns—who might run for mayor of this town or prosecutor of that county.

He was getting a feel for the place. In so many ways it was different from his home territory in the Hudson Valley. Much of the farmland was exhausted. There was hardly a paved road anywhere. So many of the people, Black and white, were living in rough little shacks with no running water and no electricity. But that was part of what fascinated him—people living in poor circumstances who might thrive with a little of the right sort of help. Like the resort at Warm Springs, the countryside of southwest Georgia struck him as a challenge. "He always tended to believe that something could be done with apparently hopeless enterprises," said a man who would come to know him well. "The more difficult the problem, it often seemed, the more the satisfaction in maneuvering for improvement."

———— ♦ ————

Eleanor said her husband hardly went anywhere new without conceiving a desire to buy land and start building something. He knew she was right. "I sometimes wish I could find some spot on the globe where it was not essential and necessary for me to start something new," he wrote a friend. "A sand bar in the ocean might answer, but I would probably start building a sea wall around it and digging for pirate treasure in the middle."

The new idea sprouting in his mind was grander than simply buying land.

He felt as if he had dropped by accident into the middle of a wildly successful medical experiment that no one else knew about. The results were right there in the pool. In just a few weeks, the people who had turned up at the train station were unquestionably doing better. FDR tallied the results. Elizabeth Retan, the young woman from Boston, had "improved remarkably."

The nineteen-year-old from Alabama had "improved much in 3 weeks." Even without exercising every day, a rebellious boy from New York had "undoubtedly improved." Mrs. Steiger reported movement in muscles where there had been none at all before. Fred Botts had seen "really extraordinary" changes. Even the most severely disabled patient—the man from Wisconsin who had overexercised too soon after his infection—was reporting a bit of progress in his toes and hamstring muscles. As for FDR himself, he cited his "rough and ready measure" of progress. The previous fall, he could stand without support in water that reached the tops of his shoulders. After making no more progress over the winter, he had exercised every day for six weeks at Warm Springs, and now he could stand with his shoulders four inches out of the water. This, he said, proved that "*all* [his] muscles had undoubtedly strengthened."

FDR and the enthusiastic young Dr. Johnson had been talking. What if Warm Springs could be built up as an actual medical center devoted to the treatment of people with polio? In the short term, he wrote one of his doctors back in New York, "It is absolutely essential that the place have a doctor and 'exercise lady.'" In the long run, "the place offers a wonderful opportunity for polyo [*sic*] cases from all parts of the country." Some six hundred letters in all had reached him. If that many people had responded to a single newspaper story, surely there were thousands of Americans in need of the waters at Warm Springs.

———◆———

Basil O'Connor thought the world of FDR. But when FDR started to talk about some big new idea, O'Connor, like Louis Howe, took it as part of his job to throw cold water on it.

So it was when Roosevelt asked O'Connor to meet with the attorney of George Foster Peabody.

Technically, Peabody did not own Warm Springs, but he had paid a sum of money to keep anyone else from buying it while he made up his mind. The price tag set by the owner was $100,000. Peabody's lawyer told O'Connor that if anyone wanted to buy Warm Springs right now, it would cost twice that figure. And $200,000 was about two-thirds of all the money FDR had.

What did O'Connor think? FDR wanted to know.

O'Connor practically laughed out loud. Was Roosevelt crazy? Buy a falling-down resort a thousand miles from home and try to turn it into a treatment center for a bunch of cripples?

But FDR was falling in love with the idea of owning Warm Springs.

"It does something for me," he said.

All that summer and fall of 1925, he kept thinking about it.

Chapter 10

"THE ONE AND ONLY TOPIC OF CONVERSATION"

Again and again, FDR had listened and nodded as Dr. Robert Lovett explained why he *must* wear his metal braces whenever he stood up to exercise or to walk with his crutches. Braces were substitutes for failing muscles, Lovett said. They protected bones and joints from pressure, strain, and fatigue, and they kept limbs in their proper alignment. When polio patients exercised without braces, it made weak muscles even weaker and pushed bones out of their proper alignment. Dr. Lovett was well aware that braces were unpleasant. But wearing them was a lot better than suffering the damage they prevented.

FDR had obeyed orders. He had submitted to being measured for braces, and when one pair didn't fit just right, he would be measured for another. He wore them when he had to. He knew they were essential to the only kind of walking he could manage right now.

But he detested those braces.

Jimmy Roosevelt said later, "He hated putting them on in the morning and he hated taking them off at night."

To get the braces on, he would sit in his underwear on the edge of his bed. LeRoy Jones or some other helper would place the braces next to him with the belts, straps, and laces open. FDR would put his hands at his sides and push his buttocks up off the bed, then hitch himself sideways and lower himself into the big heavy belt at the waist. Then four sets of straps had to be buckled—at the hips, thighs, knees, and calves. Then—again, with another person's help—his trousers had to be pulled up his legs over the braces. Next, he had to lift himself off the bed so the trousers could be pulled all the way up. At his feet, the braces were attached to specially designed shoes.

Once they were on, it felt as if his legs were trapped in metal cages. In warm weather his skin sweated under the thick leather straps. No matter how well designed, straps and metal rubbed against his skin and pressed into his flesh, which was just as susceptible to pain as ever. The braces rubbed so much they wore holes in his pants. When he felt the natural instinct to shift his weight, the braces pushed back.

Then there was the symbolism. One writer who went through polio, Paul K. Longmore, said the sight of braces on a polio patient reminded people of what they "fear most: limitation and dependence, failure and incapacity, loss of control, loss of autonomy, at its deepest level, confinement within the human condition, subjection to fate."

When the time came to take them off, he went through the routine in reverse. He would sit on the bed and hoist his buttocks up so that his trousers could be pulled off. Then the straps would be undone. Then he would heave himself up and out as his helper pulled the braces out from under him. At last his legs would be out of their cages, but just as useless as ever.

With anyone who would listen—Eleanor, his mother, Howe, Dr. Draper— he tried to argue the braces did more harm than good. After one meeting with Dr. Lovett, he came away believing—or *wanting* to believe—the doctor had finally given him permission to use the braces only when they were convenient. Some weeks later, when Eleanor mentioned to Dr. Lovett that FDR had all but abandoned the braces, Lovett told her he was "horrified." So FDR grudgingly resumed what he called "the strenuous life" and submitted to the daily indignity and discomfort of the braces. But he kept saying his exercises would do more good if his legs were free.

Then, in the summer of 1925, Fred Delano told him about a neurologist—a doctor who specializes in diseases of the nervous system, including polio—who was running an unusual program for polio patients in Marion, Massachusetts, not far from where Louis Howe had a cabin on the beach at Buzzards Bay. The doctor's name was William McDonald. Until recently he had practiced medicine in Providence, Rhode Island, and taught at the Yale Medical School. In August, FDR, Howe, and LeRoy Jones piled into a car and went to have a talk with the doctor.

In Marion they were greeted by a peppery little man who acted and spoke like the spark-plug coach of a baseball team. He insisted that FDR call him "Billie," and FDR liked him right away. He was "a peach," FDR told Dr. Draper. "Talks your language and mine!"—which meant McDonald endorsed bigger, bolder goals for his patients than the sober, cautious Dr. Lovett. In no time, FDR was calling him Billie.

McDonald explained his methods. He worked with only four patients at a time, he said. He coached them through weeks of intensive exercises, some in the water, some on an apparatus of his own invention called a "walking board." This was a rectangular platform of wooden planks, posts, and rails where patients stood upright and pulled themselves around and around for periods of an hour or more—*without braces*. He was "hot against them," FDR reported.

McDonald had a theory. Lovett and most other experts prescribed exercises for just one set of damaged muscles at a time. Those exercises were fine, McDonald said, but he also wanted his patients to exert *all* the damaged muscles at the *same* time, in coordination with each other. McDonald's idea was that braces gave the muscles too much help. Take the braces away and the muscles would have to work harder, and the patient would progress much faster toward the goal of normal movement.

In FDR's case, that might mean *walking*—without crutches, canes, or braces. It was the goal Dr. Lovett had never endorsed. Unlike Lovett, who had thought no patient could hope to walk again after two years of paralysis, McDonald had "no hard and fast opinions about the restoring of function in polio cases." Here was a doctor who believed!

McDonald gave FDR a stern warning: The exercise program would demand every bit of his stamina. But that only made it more appealing to FDR, especially when McDonald said he had "certainly succeeded in dozens of cases." The doctor recounted the case of a young woman who had been paralyzed below the waist for years, yet after two months in McDonald's care, she could stand and walk with a crutch on one side and an assistant on the other. As for FDR's own case, "he swears he can put me on my feet," FDR told Dr. Draper, "and it's worth trying."

So he asked McDonald to take him on as a patient right away. The doctor already had his full slate of four patients, but he agreed. FDR would come back in a few days and stay for four weeks. It was "a grand plan," he wrote his mother.

It wouldn't be cheap, and Eleanor may have objected to the cost. Or Franklin may have felt it would be wrong to ask her to approve spending still more on doctors' bills. In any case, he told Louis Howe to gather some of his valuable nautical prints and books and send them down to New York to be auctioned off to the highest bidder. FDR treasured his collections. But if selling them could help him walk, he was perfectly willing to let them go.

He had been paralyzed for four years now. Even at Warm Springs, further recovery of his muscles was bound to be slow. He was desperate to try something that might work fast.

———— ◆ ————

He arrived in the old whaling village of Marion at the end of August with three assistants—Missy, LeRoy Jones, and a young man he had brought up from Warm Springs. They moved into a cottage lent by the relative of an old friend.

To FDR, Marion looked much like Fairhaven, Massachusetts, just ten miles away, where his mother's ancestors had made their fortune in shipping a century earlier. FDR had spent many pleasant days in the old Delano homestead there, now owned by his uncle Fred. In that house on Thanksgiving Day in 1903, he had told his mother of his engagement to Eleanor. Like Fairhaven, Marion was a cozy village of narrow streets and saltbox houses weathered by decades of sea breezes. At 99 Water Street, Dr. McDonald's Cape Cod house backed right up to the calm waters of a secluded harbor. Wavelets lapped at an old stone pier. The sound of flapping sails came across the water. It was the sort of place where FDR felt most at home.

He quickly settled into McDonald's daily routine. In the morning, he did ninety minutes of swimming exercises like the ones at Warm Springs; in the afternoon, exercises on parallel bars under McDonald's direct supervision; then workouts of thirty minutes or more on the doctor's walking board. With no braces on his legs, he would grip the rails and haul himself back and forth, demanding that his legs share the burden of his weight with his muscular arms and shoulders.

At the end of four weeks FDR wrote Dr. Draper: "I don't hesitate to say that this treatment has done wonders—so much so that I can now get within a very few pounds of bearing my whole weight on my legs without braces."

That was just his own rough estimate, of course. It was hard to say just how many pounds he still had to go before he could stand and walk without braces—and without leaning on the heavy rails of the walking board.

But he was so sure he was making real progress that he decided to spend two more months with McDonald.

"This time I think I have hit it," he wrote Van Lear Black. "Dr. McDonald has gone one step further than the others and his exercises are doing such wonders that I expect in the course of another 10 days to be able to stand up without braces. What I did before in the way of swimming at Warm Springs was all to the good, but now I begin to see actual daylight ahead."

Day after day he kept at it. The breezes off the bay turned too cold for him to get in the water, but he worked and worked on the walking board.

He welcomed all the company he could get. Missy and Louis Howe came and went. Eleanor visited. So did his mother. They would sit nearby as he did his rounds of exercises, talking the days away.

On several October afternoons he had the company of a friend he had known since childhood, when she had been Bertie Pruyn, the daughter of a friend of his father's from Albany. Now she was Bertie Hamlin, a journalist who had married another member of Woodrow Wilson's White House circle. The Hamlins owned a summer place nearby. Like Daisy Suckley, Bertie was someone with whom FDR could reminisce about their Dutch ancestors in the Hudson Valley, and they could trade news of politics, too.

She had clear memories of Franklin in the years before polio, first as a friendly boy who had been more daring than she and her brother at sledding on snowy slopes; then as "a most attractive young man" at Harvard; and finally as a neighbor in Washington, D.C. She had an especially clear recollection of a moment when she had seen FDR running up a long slope to catch a train, "a splendid, athletic young man in his prime."

Now she saw her friend in his new condition, "very broad-shouldered and heavy" above the waist, but with legs altogether different from what she remembered.

FDR told the Hamlins he had been overdoing his exercises, and as a result one of his knees had locked up, so now he was doing additional exercises to get it working properly again. They sat and talked as he worked on the walking board. "For two or three hours . . . he talked and laughed and dragged his legs after him . . . never a word of regret or complaint from him."

Early in December 1925, FDR began to pack for the trip home to New York. He had been with Dr. McDonald at Marion for more than three months.

Slowly, cautiously, he had been practicing walking with crutches and a brace on only his left leg, and no assistants. Now, as a final test, he set off down Water Street to see how far he could go on his own.

One house.... two houses ... three houses ...

He kept going.

Dr. McDonald, LeRoy Jones, and Mrs. McDonald trailed just behind, ready to catch him if he started to fall.

Finally he made it to the edge of the wharf, nearly a block from McDonald's house. He lifted his head and cried: "I can walk!"

He called for a photograph. He slung his arms around the shoulders of Jones and McDonald. As Mrs. McDonald prepared to snap the shutter of her camera, FDR's face broke into as broad a grin as he had shown the roaring crowds at Madison Square Garden, where his hope of returning to politics had been reborn.

———————◆———————

In December 1925, all the Roosevelts came together at Hyde Park. No snow had fallen since the first day of the month, but inside the house, Christmas was blooming. FDR could no longer forage in the woods to find the family's Christmas tree, as he had done every December before polio. But he supervised the placement of the tree in the long, high-ceilinged library and the affixing of candles in its branches. (A pail of water was always kept nearby in case the tree caught fire.)

On Christmas Eve, snow began to fall, and by the next night a two-inch blanket covered the house, the lawn, and the woods. People who worked for Sara on the estate brought their children to come inside the house and see the towering tree. Later FDR performed his annual reading of Charles

Dickens's *A Christmas Carol*, "soaring into the higher registers for . . . Tiny Tim," Elliott remembered, "then shifting into a snarly imitation of mean old Scrooge." ("You know," he once told a friend, "I like to read aloud—I would almost rather read to somebody than read to myself.")

The members of the family had been scattered for months. FDR had spent much more of 1925 in Florida, Georgia, and Massachusetts than he had in New York. Eleanor was mixing her teaching role at the girls' school she had helped start in New York City with her travels as an important figure in state politics and women's affairs. Anna had been away at Cornell University for part of the year. During the school terms, James and Elliott had been at Groton School; then they'd spent the summer at a ranch in Wyoming. They'd barely seen their father in a year.

In late October, FDR arranged to be driven from Dr. McDonald's place up to Groton to watch Jimmy play in a football game. But he allowed no time to sit and talk with Jimmy and Elliott. He couldn't even join the other parents on the sidelines. "Will arrive about 2 p.m. & have to go back right afterwards," he wrote Jimmy. "Also please tell the Police Force to let me have a parking space where I can see from the car!"

Supervised by more governesses, the youngest boys were often lonesome, as a forlorn string of notes written by Franklin Jr. shows.

Dear Father,
I hope you are well. I hope you are coming up here soon...John wants mother to come next week with you.

Dear Mother and Father,
I hope you are well. The night that John came here he cried for you. I hope that you are coming soon.

Dear Father,
I hope you are having a good time down south.

All through the busy days and nights of the holidays, FDR pondered a deeply important decision. He had told George Foster Peabody he was considering whether to buy the entire compound at Warm Springs. Now Peabody was waiting for his friend's decision.

Down in Georgia, Tom Loyless was in the last stages of cancer. Soon the resort would lose the guiding spirit who had kept the place going.

That was one good reason *not* to buy Warm Springs. Without Loyless, who would run the place day to day and all year round?

There were other good reasons not to buy.

The purchase price, to start with. FDR would have to hand over roughly $200,000, the equivalent of two-thirds of all his holdings in stocks, bonds, and cash, most of it inherited from his father. He lived as if he were a rich man, but that was because his mother supplied the homes where he and his family resided. He had nothing like the resources of such truly wealthy friends as Van Lear Black or Vincent Astor. Buying Warm Springs would be an enormous financial risk.

Then would come the huge and difficult job of turning the resort into a full-fledged treatment center. New buildings and roads would be needed. Doctors and physical therapists would have to be hired. That would be long-term work. But polio patients were asking for treatment immediately. Even Loyless, who cared deeply about the place, was depressed by the people begging for help. "We have nothing to offer them," he wrote FDR at one low point, "nothing to give them in the way of proper treatment—just groping blindly in the dark and trusting to luck." How could they help these people while turning the place upside down to rebuild it?

FDR certainly didn't need to buy Warm Springs just to do his exercises there. He knew that Peabody could probably keep the place going without FDR as owner. He could visit as often as he wanted. He would have more time for exercise if he *didn't* buy the place.

But the more FDR thought about the compound, the bigger it grew in his mind's eye—bigger in what it might mean for people with polio, bigger in what it might mean for himself, too.

He wanted to *run* things, to be in charge. He had never been able to run something entirely on his own—not in the state legislature or the Navy Department or Fidelity & Deposit or his law firms. Warm Springs would be just *his*. He could rebuild the place and shape the programs exactly as he wanted.

He understood the financial risk, but he believed the place could make money. He had spent plenty of time in Florida by now, and he had seen well-to-do northerners flocking south to follow the sun as the state's economy boomed and long-distance travel beckoned to those who could afford it. Why couldn't Warm Springs become a famous way-station for some of those travelers, he wondered. He was thinking it might appeal to two different sorts of visitors—people who had polio, who would come for physical therapy, plus vacationers coming for golf, hiking, and relaxation. He could do good for the cause of fighting polio and do well at the bank, too. He cared very little for amassing money for its own sake, but he longed for the freedom money could give him. Quietly he wished he could be free of his mother's financial support and the power it gave her to interfere in his life. Warm Springs might just break him loose.

Then there was politics.

He had not been in Georgia long before he was arranging casual get-togethers with the state's most powerful Democrats. In the 1920s the southern states were the party's foundation, the so-called Solid South. Southern voters had gone for the Democrats in every presidential election since the Civil War. Any Democrat running for president had to earn the affections of that southern base. So wouldn't it be fine if this aristocratic Yankee—not the sort of politician who naturally appealed to rural southerners—could say he'd made a second home in the heart of Dixie, and developed a fine humanitarian enterprise to help poor invalids rise up and walk? It might not be the main reason to buy Warm Springs, but it was certainly another good one.

So Warm Springs was not just a place where he might get his legs in better shape. It was also a place where the terrible blow he had suffered in 1921 might be transformed into something wonderful. Perhaps thousands of people would get a second chance they would never have had if he had never been stricken. By rebuilding Warm Springs, he could show the world what a paralyzed person could do.

And it might just help him become president.

So, shortly after New Year's Day 1926, he met with George Peabody and talked over the terms of a sale. Then FDR composed a telegram to Tom Loyless, now in the final days of his life:

HAVE TALKED TO PEABODY AND AM ENCOURAGED TO THINK THAT AT LAST YOU AND I WILL SEE OUR DREAM CARRIED OUT.

———————◆———————

Sara Roosevelt was against it. Basil O'Connor was against it. Eleanor was touched to see how deeply her husband wanted to own Warm Springs. But she, too, resisted the decision. Surely it would be wiser and easier, they all thought, to devise some way of doing warm-water therapy close to home, and without risking so much money.

"I know how you love creative work," Eleanor wrote to him. "My only feeling is that Georgia is somewhat distant for you to keep in touch with what is really a big undertaking. One cannot, it seems to me, have *vital* interests in widely divided places, but that may be because I'm old and rather overwhelmed by what there is to do in one place and it wearies me to think of even undertaking to make new ties." (That was ironic coming from Eleanor, who juggled as many ties and responsibilities as FDR did.)

Her objections hurt his feelings, and she didn't hold out for long.

"He feels . . . that he's trying to do a big thing which may be a financial success & a medical and philanthropic opportunity for infantile," she wrote to a close friend, "& that all of us have raised our eyebrows & thrown cold water on it. There is nothing to do but to make him feel one is interested."

Loyless died in March. By then FDR had made an irrevocable promise to purchase Warm Springs.

It was an enormous commitment, both financial and moral. People who came to the resort for help would now depend on his ability to keep the place alive. From this point on, he would have to consider his obligations for Warm Springs—and to those deeply hopeful people—in every decision he made.

———————◆———————

In his first seven days as owner, he started at least seven major projects.

He drew up a plan for moving buildings.

He bought trees to fill the compound with greenery.

He gave orders to refurbish the Meriwether Inn.

He called contractors to see about a new water and sewage system.

He sketched a map of new roads and an artificial fishing pond.

He worked up a campaign to raise money for new buildings.

He organized a committee to plan sports and recreation indoors and outdoors.

And he saw to it that a certain rowdy contingent of locals known for "unseemly conduct at weekly dances, drinking, and carousing" were invited to "save themselves trouble by remaining away from Warm Springs."

Anna, now nineteen and about to be married, came down to get a look at her father's new domain. His enthusiasm amused and delighted her. "The one & only topic of conversation" at Warm Springs, she wrote her mother, "is *Warm Springs!*"

To attract polio patients over the long term, he would have to prove the water was special. Claims for miraculous water cures were a dime a dozen, and he was a politician, not a scientist. He needed doctors to back up his claims.

So it was something of a miracle when he learned that just then, in nearby Atlanta, the American Orthopedic Association was about to hold its spring 1926 convention. Bone doctors from all over the country would be there—he could get their backing! So he dashed off a telegram asking if he could speak to the group. Wouldn't they jump at the chance to support an extraordinary new treatment for polio?

The answer came back: *No, thank you.* The schedule was full, and it was for experts only.

Quite undaunted, FDR raced over to Atlanta. Within a couple of hours, a roomful of startled doctors found themselves shaking hands with the recent Democratic nominee for vice president, who was being pushed around the room in a wheelchair and telling them about all the extraordinary things he was doing for polio patients at a backwoods village they'd never heard of.

The president of the orthopedists' group was plainly irritated. He wrote to a friend: "I thought it was pretty clear that Mr. Roosevelt was more interested in the advertisement of his property in Georgia . . . than he was in idealism and philanthropy."

But now came another stroke of luck. At the conference there was a doctor named Robert Osgood, who had replaced Robert Lovett as head of ortho-pedics at Children's Hospital in Boston. (Lovett had died suddenly on a trip to Europe.) Dr. Osgood knew all about Roosevelt's case, and he urged his colleagues to join him in calling for a scientific study of FDR's claims. Three orthopedists agreed to review any evidence that might be gathered.

FDR was delighted. He wrote immediately to a doctor he knew back home—Leroy Hubbard, the chief orthopedic surgeon in New York State's Department of Public Health. Hubbard had been treating polio patients since 1917, and was nearly as well known in the field as Dr. Lovett had been. "I am confident that Warm Springs can be made useful," FDR told Hubbard. "The need for it is so imperative. I want to get your ideas."

Hubbard soon agreed to set aside his work in New York and travel to Georgia, where he would supervise polio patients in a study of therapeutic treatments in the special water. If, as FDR expected, Hubbard could prove that warm-water therapy brought marked improvements, then FDR would turn over the evidence to his panel of experts. And then, as he told one of the doctors, "if you gentlemen are thoroughly and 100% convinced that it is worthwhile," he would take the next step in his plan—to raise several hundred thousand dollars to construct new buildings and pools to treat one hundred patients by the summer of 1927.

Until now, no one could say for sure whether FDR had been reporting real improvements in his legs or just a pleasant fantasy born of desperate optimism. Was the pool really just an agreeable place to take a bath? Or was it the means of changing lives?

When Dr. Hubbard's survey of patients was done, they would know.

———— ◆ ————

He was now so busy at Warm Springs that he hardly had time to do what he had come there for in the first place.

Every day he had bundles of mail to go through, letters to dictate to Missy, checks to write, contractors to see, long-distance calls to make, telegrams to send, sewer diagrams to study, building plans to approve, facts to check, townspeople to reassure, doctors to consult, patients to advise. To make sure the compound remained un-fancy and rustic, as he insisted it must be, he dictated every detail of the planning. Each cottage was to be painted white; no cottage would have more than two bedrooms; and not a single road was to be paved. He jotted his own list of the purchases needed to furnish the remodeled Meriwether Inn:

```
Beds 26 @ $30 [per bed]

Dressers 26 @ $28

Writing tables 50 @ $3

Bedroom Chairs 26 @ $6

Dining Room Dishes, Silver, Glass $2,000
```

Anna was watching her father closely, assessing his physical abilities. She noticed that since she'd last spent time with him at Christmas, he'd learned some new little tricks to "handle himself better," such as shifting from a wheelchair to a chair more easily, and she saw him get up two steps without help—a significant improvement. But in spite of all his talk about how much the water at Warm Springs could help him, Anna didn't see him get into it much.

"Ma," she wrote to Eleanor, "it's awfully hard to tell whether father is walking better or not. He doesn't walk very much, & doesn't exercise overmuch."

He was simply too busy. He had sacrificed most of his money to buy the place, and now he was sacrificing most of his time to make the place work.

And he had received bad news about his legs.

One of the orthopedists he'd met in Atlanta was Dr. LeRoy Abbott, of St. Louis, Missouri. FDR told him about Billie McDonald's belief that polio patients could recover faster and walk better if they performed strenuous exercises without braces.

Dr. Abbott was appalled. Yes, FDR might well walk sooner if he followed McDonald's advice, the doctor said—but in the process he might well ruin the bones of his legs. Damaged muscles *must* be carefully built back up before the bones and joints could stand up to strenuous exertion. "He is entirely 'off' Dr. McDonald now," Anna told Eleanor.

So much for FDR's joyous shout at Dr. McDonald's place in Massachusetts: "I can walk!"

He couldn't walk—not in the sense of hopping out of a car and setting off free and easy, with no braces, crutches, or canes, the way you'd expect any politician to do.

He wasn't even close.

Chapter 11

THREE STRATEGIES

So why did he keep saying that soon he'd be walking on his own?

No doctors were saying it, except maybe Dr. McDonald. Dr. Draper, Dr. Hubbard, and the others he had consulted certainly advised more exercise. But they knew by now his chances of walking without aid had essentially dropped to zero.

Didn't he know that himself?

After all, FDR was a realist. His uncle Fred had told him years ago that wisdom lay in "taking things as they are, analyzing the facts, above all not *fooling* yourself." The Roosevelts and the Delanos believed in the power of perseverance, but they didn't believe in miracles.

Yet month after month, FDR kept telling friends and associates he expected soon to discard his braces, his crutches, possibly even his cane—when the plain fact after five years was that his legs were still far too weak to hold him.

We can never be sure why he promised himself and others what could never be. But we can make some educated guesses.

First, he seems to have told people he would walk again simply because he believed it *had* to be true. He could not concede that he was stuck in those braces. To say that would be to give up the way he had thought of himself since college—as a man like Uncle Ted, bound for the White House.

As he saw it, a successful politician not only *was* healthy (as FDR was in every sense except his mobility) but *looked* and *seemed* healthy. Yet his body shouted to observers that he was "crippled." To get up or down stairs he still had to be carried. When he walked in the only way he could, the observer saw a man in an awkward struggle with his own body. When he got in or out of a car, others found it hard to watch. For some people it was even hard to watch him get up from a chair. No one was rude enough to say so. But it was true, and FDR knew it better than anyone. He was the one who saw people's expressions change when he moved around, or look away entirely, unable to suppress their embarrassment and discomfort.

So he would not surrender to the limp muscles of his legs. If he was going to be president, he simply must not look crippled. He had to walk, so he would.

He also thought that *saying* he would walk again—and believing it—could help make it so. "It's the mind that matters, anyhow," he'd told a reporter. He followed the advice he had given his own "patients" at Warm Springs: "You've got to *know* you're going to improve." He once told a doctor that to help any polio patient, he must encourage "belief on the patient's part that the muscles are coming back." The smallest improvement in a knee, a calf, or an ankle might prove to the mind of that patient that he would come all the way back, given enough time. He assured the same doctor that "there are cases known in Norway where adults have taken the disease and not been able to walk until after a lapse of 10 or even 12 years." If those Norwegians could do it, why couldn't he? He'd been trying for only five years! He was young! He had time!

That leads to the final, and maybe the most important, reason he told people he would soon be "back on his feet." It had to do with calculations of timing.

FDR and Louis Howe were playing a cautious game of chess with the politicians of the state of New York, and in this game, timing was everything.

The king at the center of the chessboard was Al Smith. He had lost his bid for the Democratic nomination for president in 1924, but now he was running far ahead in the race to snatch that prize in 1928. This was partly because his voice was the strongest in opposition to Prohibition, the national ban on all sales of liquor, beer, and wine. After half a decade of that "noble experiment," as its supporters called it, most people thought its "noble" days were over and the experiment had failed. It seemed to have done little more than spawn a gigantic campaign of crime waged by gangsters who were selling liquor illegally. The great immigrant neighborhoods in the nation's big cities, heavily Catholic, were beginning to outnumber the Protestant farm belts and small towns in population. Governor Smith was the hero of those immigrant masses. The Democratic Party was swinging their way, and his. No other Democrat looked strong enough to challenge him. The party saw 1928 as Al's turn for the nomination.

FDR knew all this and had signed on as a loyal Smith man for 1928. But that was for public consumption. His private calculations were a little more complicated.

When FDR and Howe studied the chessboard in 1926, they considered three possible strategies:

Strategy #1: FDR could run for president right away, in 1928, leaping over the stepping-stone of statewide office. After all, a lot of Democrats back in 1924 had told Roosevelt they would back him the next time around.

But this strategy would be terribly risky. Since 1920, FDR had built a reputation as a Smith man. If he challenged Smith for the 1928 nomination, not only would he be likely to lose, but also he would brand himself as a turncoat against the party's leader.

(Actually, there *was* one narrow path to the 1928 nomination. If the Democrats got locked in a civil war like the one they'd fought in 1924, with the "wet" forces, who wanted to get rid of Prohibition, against the "dry" forces, who wanted to keep it, Smith might be pushed out of the running. If that happened, Louis Howe wrote in a confidential note, then FDR stood an "excellent chance . . . of being at least one of—if not *the* one—among the leaders who all turned to." But in 1926 Smith looked so strong that this was only a long shot—*very* long.)

Strategy #2: FDR could run for the U.S. Senate in 1926, challenging the Republican who then held the seat, James Walcott Wadsworth. If FDR won, the statewide victory would boost his prestige and his national profile, and he could bide his time in the Senate, waiting for the best year to run for president.

But the Senate strategy had its dangers, too. New Yorkers had already elected Senator Wadsworth twice. If FDR challenged him and lost, how could he run for president after that? Then there was this: A seat in the U.S. Senate offered prestige, yes, but for a politician whose ultimate aim was the White House, it was a place of peril. This is why: As a senator, FDR would have to vote on major national policies. The Democrats were split between progressives in the cities and conservatives in the countryside. On any major measure, a "yes" vote would make enemies in one faction, while a "no" vote would make enemies in the other. FDR wanted as few enemies as possible. Anyway, it was hard for a newcomer to make a mark in the Senate, with only one vote out of 96 and no seniority.

And, of course, if he ran for office now, in 1926, there was the problem of campaigning with braces, canes, and crutches. His legs weren't ready.

Strategy #3: Prepare for the right year to run for governor of New York.

This strategy had many advantages.

FDR loved the state of New York and liked the idea of being its leader.

He was a born executive, not a legislator. He wanted to be the one in charge.

He knew the governorship could be a stepping-stone to the White House, as it had been for Uncle Ted.

And FDR wanted not just to be president but to be a *great* president. He needed experience, and he knew it.

You could look at it as a simple matter of odds—of statistical probabilities—which Louis Howe had been calculating since his days around the horse-racing tracks of Saratoga Springs.

These were the numbers:

Since the Civil War, the Democratic Party had nominated thirteen men for president. Of those thirteen, seven had been New Yorkers, and three of those men had been governor. One, his father's friend Grover Cleveland, had been elected president in two different years, 1884 and 1892. The Republicans had nominated two New York governors for president, and one of them—Uncle Ted—had reached the White House. (He'd succeeded to the presidency when President William McKinley was assassinated in 1901, but he'd been elected in his own right in 1904.)

New York, with 10 percent of the U.S. population and 17 percent of the electoral votes needed to win the presidency, was the biggest state in the Union by far. If you could run the government of New York, with its gigantic metropolis and its sprawling reaches of upstate farm country, it was pretty clear you could run the government of the whole country.

Anyone who hopes to be president faces long odds. But a smart gambler would look favorably upon any governor of New York.

When to run? The next election year, 1928, looked promising. If Smith won the White House in that year and FDR became governor, FDR could build a strong record as chief executive of the Empire State and run for president in 1932 or 1936.

And if Smith *lost* in 1928, he would likely be finished as a national candidate and out of FDR's way for good.

So at this point, Strategy #3 looked like the right one.

If he could walk.

A friend in the Democratic Party—a wealthy upstate New York brewer named Louis B. Wehle—had recently written to FDR about the political outlook in strictest confidence.

Wehle said he knew FDR would be supporting Governor Smith for the nomination in 1928. But he asked FDR to permit "your friends . . . to organize the situation in your behalf in the event that Smith should not receive the nomination."

Between the lines, FDR could read Wehle's intentions. His friend wanted to spread the word—very quietly—that FDR was ready to step in if Smith's momentum toward the nomination could be blocked.

But FDR wrote back and said no, he couldn't allow it—or rather, his legs wouldn't allow it.

"I must give principal consideration for at least 2 years more to getting back the use of my legs," he told Wehle. "Up to now I have been able to walk only with great difficulty with steel braces and crutches, having to be carried up and down steps, in and out of cars, etc., etc. Such a situation is, of course, impossible in a candidate.

"I am, however, gaining greatly and hope, within a year, to be walking without the braces, with the further hope of then discarding the crutches in favor of canes and eventually possibly getting rid of the latter also. The above are necessarily only hopes, as no human being can tell whether the steady improvement will keep up."

Those few sentences perfectly summed up the strategy that FDR and Louis appear to have chosen—the best strategy to secure a position of strength on that complicated chessboard.

In one sense, FDR meant just what he said. He hoped before too long to be walking with only a cane, and if he accomplished that, he could run for office. He wasn't ready now, but he could be soon.

This was the plain truth. But the truth served his deeper purposes, too.

He hoped that this not-now-but-later strategy would prevent Democratic friends like Wehle from pressuring him to mount a direct challenge to Smith for the party's next presidential nomination. It would also repel any pressure to run for the U.S. Senate. Howe reminded him of that on the eve of the New York Democratic Party's 1926 convention. FDR had agreed to nominate Smith for another two-year term as governor. Then the party would choose its Senate nominee.

"I hope your spine is still sufficiently strong to assure them that you are still nigh to death's door for the next two years," Howe warned FDR. "Please try and look pallid and worn and weary when you address the convention so it will not be too exceedingly difficult to get by with the statement that your health will not permit you to run for anything for 2 years more."

But it was risky to look *too* "worn and weary." If that was how he appeared, Democratic leaders in New York might just write Roosevelt off for good. That was why he had to hold out the tantalizing promise of a full comeback.

FDR and Howe were saying to each other: *Just stay in the game . . . Don't let their attention wander too far, or other men may pass you by . . . Meanwhile, pursue recovery by every available method.*

That consideration—the delicate business of timing his return to politics at just the right moment—seems to be the final reason he kept telling people that he expected to be so much better . . . soon.

Did he mean it? Good question.

Of course, sometimes he didn't tell the truth at all.

"I honestly have no desire either to run for the presidency or to be president," he remarked to a reporter about this time. "I have seen much of presidents and administrations. Even though it may sound selfish, I would rather do my bit as a private in the ranks."

———— ◆ ————

On an overcast day in June 1926, Anna Roosevelt, who had just turned twenty, was married to Curtis Dall, her senior by nine years, at St. James Episcopal Church, a lovely stone sanctuary under Hyde Park's towering trees.

She was not a very happy bride. "I got married when I did because I wanted to get out," she admitted later—out of the tense circle of her family, that is, where there was seldom a thaw in the cold war between her mother and grandmother.

Sara Roosevelt had been offering her usual disapproving remarks and adding new ones—about Eleanor's political activities; about Franklin's long absences from New York; and about Eleanor's recent decision, with FDR's approval and help, to build a stone cottage, called Val-Kill, two miles from the "big house," where she and two close women friends would stay whenever they were in Hyde Park. Eleanor steamed. If she wrote Franklin about his mother's latest needling, he would return support and sympathy, then remind Eleanor that after all, she knew what Sara was like.

Still, on the wedding day, the family went through all the motions of a big, happy family celebration. They offered smiling welcomes to guests arriving from New York City on special train cars—associates of Franklin's from politics, the business world, and Harvard; friends of Eleanor's from her private school in New York and her comrades in feminist circles; people like Sara from upper-crust families in the wealthy enclaves of Newport, Rhode Island, Tuxedo Park, New York, and Manhattan's Upper East Side.

After the wedding service, the bridal party and guests were transported to the Roosevelt estate, where they spread across the lawn for refreshments and wedding cake. On such occasions, a friend said, FDR, seated in a centrally placed chair, would be "talking to everybody, bantering with his children, teasing them and they him. The youngsters would tell preposterous stories to dignified visitors to see if they could get away with them, and would burst into gales of laughter regardless of whether the visitor fell for the story or saw through them." Sara glided gracefully from one group of guests to another— "such an indomitable and exciting personality," as a friend said—while Eleanor tended to minor emergencies and looked after guests' special needs.

The guests chattered about mutual friends and social connections, of plans for travel and recreation in the coming summer—all casual, pleasant, and far removed from serious public affairs. But anyone watching closely would have seen that political calculations were not far from the mind of the bride's father, even on his daughter's wedding day.

The evidence turned up when formal photographs were taken. These photos wouldn't be just keepsakes for family albums. When the daughter of such a famous man was married, it was news, so a press photographer was on the scene, and his pictures would be sent all over the country for publication on the society pages of major newspapers.

The lead photograph shows Anna in the center of the frame in her lace wedding gown; her new husband, Curtis, tall and gangly, at the left; and at the right her father, somehow dominating the image, his broad shoulders and powerful chest filling out his tuxedo, looking remarkably strong and fit for a man who was known to have weathered an awful disease.

You had to look carefully at the photograph to see that FDR was grasping the handle of a cane in his left hand. The rest of the cane is hidden behind Anna's big German shepherd, Chief.

Why, any casual viewer would say, *he looks fit as a fiddle.*

And he was—in every way except the ability to walk on his own.

But for the moment, the important thing—to FDR and Louis Howe—was that he *looked* that way.

Chapter 12

"HE WAS GETTING READY FOR SOMETHING"

● ●

At the end of the summer of 1926, Dr. Leroy Hubbard came in for a long chat.

Hubbard was not a man like Roosevelt, who bubbled over with optimism at the slightest excuse. But two months of observation had persuaded the sober, cautious Hubbard that optimism was justified. Warm Springs appeared to be the real thing.

These were his findings:

Of the twenty-three patients he'd studied—twelve males and eleven females, ages four to forty-four—nearly all had arrived at Warm Springs as "severe" cases with little hope of getting any better. After eight weeks, almost all had achieved notable improvements in mobility. All but one had learned to swim without support. Fred Botts, the singer from Pennsylvania who had come to Warm Springs a year earlier confined entirely to a wheelchair, was now up and walking with one crutch. A twenty-two-year-old man from Massachusetts, completely paralyzed at the start of the summer, was also walking with one crutch. A fifteen-year-old girl had "improved considerably." A seven-year-old girl "walks considerably better than she did when she came." A four-year-old boy who had arrived with both legs paralyzed now walked with crutches and was "fearless in the pool."

"No miracles can be performed at Warm Springs," Dr. Hubbard would tell his fellow orthopedists. "No false hopes should be aroused in the minds of patients or their families." Yet he could say beyond a reasonable doubt that "the exercises and warm water under proper supervision give a better hope for fairly rapid improvement in muscle power than any other method with which I am familiar."

He didn't know why, exactly. Maybe the same program of exercise and instruction conducted somewhere else would bring the same sort of results. But if so, Dr. Hubbard hadn't seen it, and he'd been working with polio patients for years. Certainly there was something in the water at Warm Springs—the perfect temperature or the minerals or both—that made it easy to exercise for long periods. In fresh water most people get tired after half an hour, while at Warm Springs the patients could work out for two hours before fatigue set in. That was probably the chief factor—simply that people could exercise for much longer periods than on dry land or in cold water.

But a human factor was at work, too. The patients were helping each other. There was "a psychological effect due to each striving to equal the other in improvement," Dr. Hubbard said. "Also the fact that these boys and girls deprived of the usual sports are able in the water to rival the normal boy and girl and have a feeling that at least in one sport they can take part."

We don't know if the conversation between FDR and Dr. Hubbard turned to FDR's own case. But we do know what Dr. Hubbard believed about cases *like* FDR's, because he stated his views just a few weeks later in his formal report on Warm Springs.

Dr. Hubbard had been looking for two kinds of changes in the patients. First, did they show growing strength in tests of isolated muscle groups? Second, could they use their arms and legs more skillfully in everyday activity?

The doctor observed that the two things usually went together, but not always. He saw that some patients—especially those who had been paralyzed for years—could achieve little or no gain in strength in isolated muscle groups. But they *could* "obtain quite a considerable improvement in function"—that is, in the ability to move around. Of patients like this, he said, "very few, or perhaps none of them, can expect to come back to normal or approximately normal. The most we can hope for is such a gain in muscle power and functional activity that they can get about . . . and some of them ultimately progress enough to discard all apparatus" (that is, braces, crutches, or canes).

In other words, such people could not bring dead nerves back to life. But they *could* learn to walk much better.

As the two men talked that day, did Dr. Hubbard spell out the clear implications for FDR's own case? Maybe so, maybe not. But even if he didn't say it out loud, the meaning of Dr. Hubbard's observations must have struck FDR with full force.

It was the same thing Dr. Lovett and Dr. Draper had hinted at years earlier. FDR had been able to push the message away, believing he would be different. With the special willpower of a Roosevelt and a Delano, *he* would defy the odds, recover all his strength, and walk again as he once had. But now he was facing the results of a full-out effort to restore as much mobility as possible among people whose cases, on average, were just like his. With proper instruction, they were doing better, even much better, but they were never going to walk normally. To get better meant a lot. But as the doctor said, it was the most they could hope for.

Finally that lesson sank in, or so it seems from what happened next.

———— ♦ ————

Dr. Hubbard had recruited a physical therapist from New York to direct the exercise program at Warm Springs. She was Helena T. Mahoney, a woman who was devoted to her calling and very good at it. In the 1910s, in Boston, she had moved from nursing into the new profession of physiotherapy (soon to be called, simply, *physical therapy*), working under Dr. Lovett and Wilhelmine Wright. She began to work with polio patients soon after the great epidemic of 1916. By now she was an expert. Lately she'd been treating patients in New York with Dr. Hubbard. So it was natural for Hubbard to ask her to come down and help with his summer experiment at Warm Springs.

She made the long trip from New York by automobile, then promptly took command of the patients. She had the manner of a savvy classroom teacher, likable but strict. She was not called "Miss Mahoney" at Warm Springs, just "Mahoney."

We have only one report of the conversations Mahoney had with FDR in the last days of the summer of 1926, and we can't entirely trust it.

The account appears in a book called *Roosevelt and the Warm Springs Story*, written in the early 1950s by a writer named Turnley Walker. He was a polio survivor who had spent time at Warm Springs as a youngster. For his book, he spoke with many of the people who had worked with FDR in the early years, including Helena Mahoney.

According to Turnley Walker, Mahoney and FDR had long talks about Mahoney's experience with polio patients, including her difficult efforts simply to *find* those who'd been hidden away by their families in back bedrooms. They sketched plans for physical therapy at Warm Springs. Then they discussed FDR's own condition. Here's how the writer described the key part of that conversation:

MAHONEY: "What about your own legs, Mr. Roosevelt?"

ROOSEVELT: "I'll find my improvement with the others.

I'm not a man to accomplish much of anything alone."

MAHONEY: "Of course I know nothing about your muscle setup. How much improvement do you expect?"

ROOSEVELT: "I'll walk without crutches. I'll walk into a room without scaring everybody half to death. I'll stand easily enough in front of people so that they'll forget that I'm a cripple."

Now, that represents a significant change in FDR's mindset. He had always said he intended one day to walk on his own. With Mahoney, he was describing quite a different goal. He seemed less concerned with his ability to walk and more concerned with the effect of his appearance on others. He apparently was thinking now that perhaps he could reach the White House without making a full recovery, if only he could dispel the feelings of embarrassment and revulsion that many people felt when they encountered the disabled.

But we can't be sure that conversation really happened, at least not in those exact words.

Turnley Walker was writing at a time when many authors believed it was all right to describe historical events as if every episode, every scrap of conversation, could be re-created just as it occurred, even though that's impossible unless the events have been recorded with cameras and microphones.

Still, unless Walker made up the entire conversation between Mahoney and FDR—and that's very unlikely, since many details in *Roosevelt and the Warm Springs Story* can be corroborated by reliable documents—then it's quite possible, even probable, that a conversation much like the one Walker reported really did happen.

There are other possibilities, too.

As Helena Mahoney spoke with Turnley Walker, she may have blended memories of several conversations with FDR—or her impressions of what FDR was thinking—into the memory of a single conversation. Possibly Mahoney's memory of the conversation was shaped by her own beliefs about what Roosevelt *should* have been aiming for in his therapy—since all her professional training and values lay along those lines.

In any case, we're left with the likelihood that *something* like that conversation happened.

What we know for sure is that in the fall of 1926 and the spring of 1927, FDR acted very much as if his thinking had taken the turn Mahoney described.

He took his place with the other polio patients in the pool. He was no longer "Old Dr. Roosevelt," giving instructions. He was obeying orders from Mahoney, who began to re-introduce him to Wilhelmine Wright's teachings, all of them aimed at making the maximum possible use out of the working muscles that remained to him.

———◆———

At Warm Springs that fall there was a patient in her mid-twenties named Margaret Pope. A few years earlier she'd been a student at the University of Wisconsin and a state champion in golf. Then, at about the same time as FDR, she contracted polio and lost the use of her legs.

Margaret's father, Henry Pope, was a wealthy manufacturer of stockings in Chicago. He had joined his daughter's search for the best possible treatment. When the braces prescribed for Margaret were awkward and uncomfortable, Henry Pope assigned one of his engineers to devise new ones out of lightweight materials used in airplanes. When the Popes heard about Warm Springs, father and daughter visited early in 1926, and they, too, fell in love with the place. Pope wrote FDR afterward to say he was "regretting I cannot be with you in that beautiful pool, instead of in Chicago with a foot of snow and more falling."

People like Henry Pope—with lots of money, a personal stake in polio treatments, and even wealthier friends like Edsel Ford, son of the automotive pioneer Henry Ford—were just the sort FDR hoped to enlist as supporters of Warm Springs. So he made it a point to stay in touch. When the Popes returned to Georgia in the fall of 1926, the friendship continued, and Pope began to take an interest in FDR's own case. He considered what was immediately ahead of FDR—another cold New York winter indoors, without steady access to a heated pool and without an expert like Mahoney to coach him.

This gave Pope an idea. In Chicago, he told FDR, his daughter had been seeing a fine physical therapist named Alice Lou Plastridge, another student of Wilhelmine Wright's. Wouldn't it make sense for FDR to continue this sort of treatment over the winter in New York, perhaps with Miss Plastridge herself? He must not lose the progress he was making through another long spell of inactivity. In fact, Pope offered to pay Plastridge's fee as a token of gratitude for what FDR had already done for Margaret by establishing the center at Warm Springs.

So it was that Alice Lou Plastridge, suitcase in hand, found herself face-to-face with Sara Delano Roosevelt, who opened the big front door in Hyde Park on the day after Thanksgiving.

———————— ◆ ————————

Miss Plastridge had grown up in a small town in the Green Mountains of Vermont, about two hundred miles north of the Roosevelt estate. At Mount Holyoke College she was trained as a teacher in physical education and gymnastics, but in 1914 she took a summer course at Harvard in the treatment of scoliosis, an inherited condition that causes painful curvature of the spine. The man in charge was none other than Dr. Robert Lovett, who soon hired Plastridge to work in his clinic, where she learned physical therapy. In 1917, with many young polio patients in need of treatment, Lovett urged her to open her own practice in Chicago. Though she was only in her twenties, she became one of the first physical therapists in the city. She held to the no-nonsense tenets that she and Helena Mahoney had learned at the Lovett clinic. "It is rarely if ever too late to do constructive work, for improvement will continue for a period of years if proper treatment is given—and continued," she wrote. But "it is extremely discouraging because improvement is so slow."

When Henry Pope proposed that she spend a month with the Roosevelts in New York, she said later, "I knew at the end of five years [since the onset of FDR's paralysis] one month was a drop in the bucket." But Pope was so keen on the idea that she agreed to spend Thanksgiving through Christmas with the Roosevelts.

———————◆———————

Lovett, Wright, Mahoney, and Plastridge believed polio survivors enjoyed the right to live full, rich, independent lives to the greatest extent possible. As they plotted therapeutic strategies and tactics, the first physical therapists operated with a deeply practical understanding of everything patients were up against. It wasn't just the paralysis or weakness of a damaged muscle. It was the way people looked at them when they moved their arms or legs awkwardly, and the false conclusions people drew about those awkward movements—that polio survivors were best shut away in back rooms and sanitariums, where "normal" people wouldn't have to see them. These notions about people with disabilities were summed up by the word *stigma*, which in medieval times referred to a burn made on the skin with a hot iron, something like a tattoo, signifying disgrace. Stigma was worse than muscular weakness. It was not too far from a criminal's sentence to banishment from society.

The physical therapists knew the stigma of disability was deeply unjust, but they also knew it was powerful. They could not dispel it by themselves, and certainly not overnight, perhaps not ever. So to fight the stigma, they taught their patients how to make their movements as normal as possible.

Many years later, disabled people would start to ask: If the stigma lies in the minds of the able-bodied, why are we the ones who have to change? Why don't *they* change the way *they* think? But not in the 1920s. For the early physical therapists, learning to walk "like normal" was partly for safety and partly for speed, but it was also, as Plastridge put it, so that "limps and distorted positions shall not become conspicuous." A key aim of "corrective walking," she advised, must be "moving quietly and steadily without needless body, leg or arm motions which would attract attention to the disability."

This was Plastridge's mindset as she prepared to work with Franklin Roosevelt. It was perfectly suited to the new goal FDR had described to Helena Mahoney in Warm Springs—to "walk into a room without scaring everybody half to death."

Many years later, Plastridge remembered being received at Hyde Park as graciously as if she had been the queen of Spain. First Sara greeted her warmly, then Eleanor, then Anna. As the women moved into the spacious library, chatting as they walked, Plastridge heard a man's rich tenor voice calling from the far end of the room: "Well, aren't you ever going to come and speak to *me*?"

At Plastridge's orders, the Roosevelts once again had a long wooden slab laid across sawhorses in FDR's bedroom, and again he was helped to stretch out on the slab for daily exercises, just as he had done with Kathleen Lake five years earlier. When Plastridge got him up on his crutches, she immediately saw just how little he had learned about how to use them. In his long sessions with Dr. McDonald in Massachusetts, when the focus had been strengthening the muscles, he had all but abandoned his efforts at smoother, steadier walking with crutches and canes. He would swing the crutches far out ahead of his body and bring them crashing down with such force that she thought the floor would give way, then drag his limp legs forward by the strength of his arms and upper body alone.

After two weeks of workouts she could see no gain in strength and no improvement in his crutch-walking. "I knew we weren't getting anywhere because there wasn't any motion in his legs," she said later. "I didn't know what I was going to do."

Then one day he sat down too hard in a chair and hurt his back, leaving him in considerable pain.

When Plastridge appeared at his door the next morning, he grumbled: "What are you here for? Didn't you know I hurt my back?"

She had heard many such excuses from other patients.

"I thought maybe I could do a little work with you," she replied. "Will it hurt your back to move your toes?"

"Yes!" he shot back.

"Then you're not doing it right."

"Prove it!"

She did.

For the first time ever, FDR learned how to exert control over one isolated set of muscles at a time. With practice, he got so he could move just his toes without moving his whole foot, and he could move his foot without moving his entire leg. Control over isolated muscle groups meant greater control over his balance and coordination, which in turn might mean moving around with less risk of a fall and less awkwardness in his motions.

They spent another week on these new techniques. FDR listened as Plastridge reminded him of the principles of long-term physical rehabilitation, how the combination of practice and perseverance might lead, even after all this time, to substantial improvements in his ability to manage his movements. Each skill demanded concerted, deliberate practice. "It is like an athlete going into training," she remarked. "He must work long and hard to develop and perfect himself in his specialty."

It was a new start. FDR sensed possibilities he had not seen before. He was re-imagining the task before him, and it looked far more feasible than the impossible challenge of complete recovery.

Just before Christmas, as Plastridge was about to return to Chicago, she sat down to dinner with members of the family. A gift-wrapped box sat before her on the table. She looked at FDR.

"Open it!" he ordered.

Inside she found a gold ring with a lapis stone. It was engraved: FOR ALICE LOU PLASTRIDGE, WITH WARM REGARDS FROM HER OLD FRIEND, F.D. ROOSEVELT.

———————◆———————

On January 30, 1927, FDR turned forty-five years old. Two weeks later, he got himself off the train in Warm Springs and went back to work on all fronts.

Now that his panel of expert orthopedists had endorsed the idea of a polio treatment center at Warm Springs, he supervised the legal and financial work of organizing the Georgia Warm Springs Foundation, the nonprofit corporation that would own and operate the center. He made phone calls and held meetings to make sure the construction of his own cottage would be done soon. He met with contractors about the rehabilitation of the Meriwether Inn. He bought more land, including a lovely wooded promontory called Dowdell's Knob, where he loved to take people for picnics. He gave speeches to church groups and civic groups. Politics intruded when his new friends among the Democrats of Georgia "boomed" him for president, meaning they spread talk in the party and the press that he would make a better nominee in 1928 than Al Smith, whom the southerners feared. Once again FDR had to shut them down, insisting he could and would not be a candidate. When Missy LeHand became seriously ill, he had to make sure she received care, then arranged for her to go home for an extended rest.

Yet from February to May, he made time to practice walking with Helena Mahoney. Never since the beginning of his recovery in 1921 had he been so disciplined, and he began to see real results. In pursuit of his new and realistic goal—to walk with help while drawing as little attention as possible to his handicap—he made more concrete progress in three months than in all the years since 1921.

Mahoney studied his movements. She was interested in more than just the latest tricks in how he could best get in or out of a chair or up or down a step. She was focused on the connections between the brain's nervous system and the body—how they changed with prolonged paralysis, and how they could be restored bit by bit. "Most of us have experienced instability in walking after even a short illness," she would write. "We called it weakness, but a major part was lack of coordination and balance. [They] are elusive qualities. They must be reeducated if unused for any length of time." For the patient who has only some muscles in working order, walking is an entirely new skill. "He needs help to train unaccustomed muscles to function smoothly and spontaneously. Normal people experience some of this difficulty when learning a new game; a beginner at golf or tennis, or even at a new dance, is usually slow and awkward and only practice gives us a smooth performance.

"Just as there are what athletes call 'naturals' in sport, there are some patients who will instinctively know how to use their muscles to obtain a certain function. Others must be patiently taught to do the same thing."

FDR was one who had to be taught, and now that Mahoney understood what he could and couldn't do, she delivered. She showed him a way of moving that would attract the least possible attention to his disability while allowing him to say, as he so much wanted to, "I can walk."

We don't know exactly how she taught him the technique, but it probably started with her simply saying: "Watch this."

In her right hand she held a cane, planting the tip firmly on the floor just ahead of her. On her left side she placed an assistant, then grasped his arm just above the elbow. She kept both of her legs locked at the knees, like FDR in his braces. Then she began to rock her weight slightly to the left, then slightly to the right, just enough to pull each foot off the floor. As she rocked to the right, her left foot rose. When she rocked to the left, her right foot rose . . . just a bit, half an inch or so, enough to clear the floor. *Right . . . left . . . right . . . left again . . .* and this time, as she leaned left, she twisted her upper body slightly to the left and swung her right foot forward a few inches . . . *rock to the right, twist to the right,* and she swung the left foot forward. She was doing it with the strength of her upper body, swinging the legs like two stiff pendulums. Next to her, the assistant swayed in rhythm with her. The only difference was that he was bending his legs slightly at the knee and using the muscles below his waist to move his legs forward. But if you looked at the two of them moving together, more or less identically, they both seemed to be, well, walking.

Now you do it, she said.

Slowly, through trial and error, he began to get the hang of it. He would never be able to do it swiftly. He would never be able to jump up from a chair and hurry off across the room. He would always need at least one helper to lift him to the standing position, then walk along with him. And he would never do this without the danger that something would go wrong and he would fall, as he still did from time to time. But with a strong and well-trained aide at his side, he began to see that he could perform this athletic feat whenever he needed to show that he was not "confined to a wheelchair." He might be lame, but he could "walk like a man"—across a stage or into a room—and "without scaring everyone to death."

In later years some would say this was nothing more than a clever deception, a parlor act—that FDR could not "really walk." No, not by himself. But doctors define the act of walking with the two words *bipedal ambulation*, which means "traveling across a surface while standing upright on two feet." That's what he was doing. He just needed a little help. Thanks to Alice Lou Plastridge, Helena Mahoney, and his new willingness to bend his goals to what was truly possible, he could move about in public without a wheelchair or crutches, the symbols of being "crippled."

The more he practiced, the more graceful his sway-walking became. His natural athletic skill reasserted itself. During his exercises he could even manage to walk with just two canes, holding no one's arm, though that was too risky to do as a regular thing.

With so much exercise his muscles grew stronger. Better coordination and greater strength began to feed off each other.

As March turned to April and the warm Georgia spring came on, Mahoney, who was not easily impressed, was delighted with her patient's accomplishment. But she began to worry that he might once again squander the progress he was making once he returned home. So she wrote to Eleanor to ask for her help:

"Mr. Roosevelt is doing so very well I want you to know it. He is walking with two canes at exercise and also with my arm and a cane. His muscles are greatly improved, his knees especially are much stronger. He has never shown such interest and attention to this work since I have been here. I do dread having it interrupted and do hope he will stay just as long as possible for we always have to go back some each time he goes away. Even two weeks or so longer will help to establish what we have. We hope you will persuade Mr. Roosevelt to stay a bit longer."

Eleanor likely knew her own persuasive powers with her husband were seldom a match for Louis Howe's. So she showed the letter to Howe, who quickly urged FDR to stay on in Georgia. "I can't tell you how pleased I am, old man, at the details she gives of the way you have come back," Howe wrote. "I have always felt you would." (Here Howe may have been picturing something more like the complete recovery that FDR had wished for earlier.) "Now I'm not going to advise one way or the other because I concluded long ago that you know more about your case and what to do for it than the doctors did."

FDR did stay two weeks longer, and after a short trip home, he returned to Warm Springs for three more weeks.

Mahoney wrote again to tell Eleanor of his progress. "We are very happy to have Mr. Roosevelt back with us," she said. "I did not realize how much we needed him until I saw him and slipped the burden back to his shoulders . . . He gets his exercise every day and it is good to see him walk around the house with a crutch and cane and stand up to the table and do and get what he wants. His balance improves. I am sure you will find him doing more and more on his feet."

———————◆———————

Late in the evening of April 6, 1927, Paul Hasbrouck, a young man with polio, arrived in Warm Springs for a visit of several weeks. He was from Poughkeepsie, New York, just a few miles from Hyde Park. He and FDR had struck up a friendship. Hasbrouck, an army veteran of World War I, had been paralyzed below the waist in his mid-twenties when he was a member of the U.S. Senate's staff. He went home to live with his parents in Poughkeepsie and work on his recovery. He arranged to study for a master's degree in political science and economics from his alma mater, Hamilton College, then a Ph.D. from Columbia University—in that era, an extraordinary achievement for a person with a disability. In the spring of 1927, he had just submitted the manuscript of his first book, a study of political parties in the U.S. House of Representatives, to a major publisher. Short and very thin, he could walk haltingly with braces and canes but hoped to do much better. He and FDR had been corresponding about polio treatments off and on for several years, and FDR had urged him to come and try Warm Springs. Now, at the age of thirty-one, with his studies complete, he was ready to do so.

Hasbrouck was dropped off at one of the compound's new, long bungalow-style cottages. In back there was a screen porch with rocking chairs under a canopy of shade trees. His spacious room, plain but cheerful, had the pleasant scent of clean, fresh lumber, with brand-new linens on the bed and a new dresser and table. He went across the road to the dining room and was served a hot supper. He was eager to look the whole place over, but it was already dark, so he had to wait for morning.

He had hardly awakened when he heard the noise of trees being felled nearby, and when he got outside, he saw a tractor pushing away the logs, making way for new construction. Then carpenters began tearing the old siding off his cottage to replace it with new. Just before 10:00 A.M., Hasbrouck was picked up by car and driven with a few other patients down a sloping dirt road to the two pools—a slightly smaller one just for the polio guests, a larger one for members of the public and visitors. He met Mahoney, who struck him as "an excellent executive."

Around the pool Hasbrouck found clean, new changing rooms where each guest was presented with two fresh towels every morning, just as in a fine resort. In the air he caught a faint whiff of something like sulfur wafting up from the sparkling water. He learned the pools were emptied each evening, then scrubbed, whereupon the pipes were reopened to allow fresh water to gush in. When he lifted a handful to his mouth, it tasted not of chemicals, exactly, but decidedly "soft."

He slid into the pool and soon understood what Roosevelt had been telling him about its unusual qualities. The experience was "just splendid in every way," he said in a letter to his father. "Its temperature is mildly warm to the touch, and the whole pool stays so mild that today I stayed in for what seemed a very long time without having any desire to get out. I walk freely all over the pool." When he finally got out, he rested for a while, as patients were instructed, but "I felt so refreshed from the swimming that I had little need of rest."

Back at his cottage after lunch, Hasbrouck heard the whirring clatter of a Ford Model T pulling up outside. He looked out to see Franklin Roosevelt at the wheel, smiling his giant smile.

Hasbrouck said later it was he who had given FDR the idea of rigging up an automobile with hand controls for disabled drivers. Whether it had been his idea or someone else's—possibly FDR's own—FDR had jumped on it. During his summer visit to Warm Springs in 1926, he'd picked up an old Model T for fifty dollars and put a local mechanic to work on it. Using FDR's sketch, the mechanic attached metal rods to the foot pedals, then brought the rods up through the dashboard and capped them with handles, which FDR could push or pull to accelerate or put on the brakes. He tried it out and pronounced it a spectacular innovation. It was the first time since 1921 that he had achieved fully independent mobility, and from then on he seized every chance to drive himself and his passengers up and down the village roads and out into the countryside. At both Warm Springs and the estate at Hyde Park, he would never again be without a car he could drive.

FDR waved Hasbrouck into the car and took off down the lane to give his young friend a full tour. There was much to see—far more than when FDR first saw the property in 1924. Bulldozers were carving new roads in the red earth. From deep inside the old Meriwether Inn came the racket of carpenters. The "push boys"—local youths hired for the purpose—were taking patients in wheelchairs down to the pools, where Helena Mahoney's "physios," as the physical therapists were called, were putting patients through their demanding exercise routines and walking practice. Turf was being seeded on the golf course. In every building, whether remodeled or new, ramps were being built in place of steps and stairs.

What Hasbrouck and other newcomers saw was the construction of a place seldom seen before—a center devoted entirely to the physical and emotional well-being of people who were pitied or shunned wherever else they went. It was not a forbidding sanitarium, all white starch and somber silence, but a lively sanctuary from stigma where the patients grew accustomed to the same respect, social engagement, and just plain fun that people without disabilities could take for granted wherever they went.

"When we finished with the work at hand, we'd have what we called water polo," recalled a Georgian who served as one of the push boys. "It really wasn't water polo; it was 'try to get the ball away from Mr. Roosevelt.' He would sit in the middle of the pool . . . From the waist down he was skin and bones, but from the waist up, he was a powerful man. He'd hold that rubber ball high above his head in the air and just dare you to come and get it. Every time I'd get close, he'd take his powerful hands and push me down. When he pushed, you went straight to the bottom of the pool."

At night, people who had been pointed at with pity, even fear, on the streets of their hometowns found fresh flowers on tables set for dinner, with free-wheeling evenings of poker and bridge to follow. They competed in parlor games—how many words could be made from the letters in *C-o-n-s-t-a-n-t-i-n-o-p-l-e*?—and watched movies. There was to be a school for the younger patients, plus a clinic, a library, and shops. On cool evenings there were blazing logs in the fireplaces. Every week, auto caravans carried everyone out through the peach orchards to picnic spots. On special nights the big pool was lit for moonlit swims. Soon, engagement announcements would be seen on the big bulletin board.

It was a summer colony infused with the informal spirit of outdoor fun that Franklin Roosevelt believed in like a creed and charged with a special sense of purpose. Stronger muscles and better coordination were only part of it. The spirit of the place drew upon FDR's determination to restore hope and dignity to people who thought those essential qualities of life had been lost for good.

In 1926, he had committed his money to Warm Springs. In 1927 he gave his heart to it. It was an enterprise large enough to absorb all his attention and prodigious energy, and its people—staff and patients alike—now depended on him. He was in very deep.

But now, unlike in 1926, when Anna had watched her father doing everything *but* much exercise, he stuck to his walking practice.

In the spring of 1928, he worked a lot with a physio named Mary Hudson.

"He came every day," Hudson told the historian Geoffrey Ward many years later, "and always on time. You knew he was getting ready for something."

Hudson's examinations showed how very little muscle mass had been restored below the waist by all of Roosevelt's exercising. But with the fingers of his left hand gripping Hudson's arm and his right hand squeezing the handle of his cane, he walked and walked.

How did he do it? Geoffrey Ward asked Hudson.

She tapped her forehead.

"It's all up here," she said. "He just decided to do it. He walked on sheer determination. He was ready. It was time."

PART 4

"A TOUCH OF DESTINY"

·····························

(FALL 1928–FALL 1932)

Chapter 13

"YOU'VE GOT TO PLAY THE GAME"

• •

"I'm telling everyone you are going to Houston without crutches," Eleanor wrote him, "so mind you stick at it!"

It was the summer of 1928. He was bound for Houston, Texas. At the Democratic National Convention, he would once again nominate Al Smith for president.

And he went without crutches.

For the third time in eight years, thousands of Democrats in a sweltering arena watched him advance to center stage at the Democratic National Convention. In 1920 in San Francisco he had been young, quick, and strong. In 1924 at Madison Square Garden he had been thin, shaky, and slow. Now, in 1928, the delegates saw yet another version of Franklin Roosevelt. He was still slow and obviously lame. But he was walking more confidently than he had four years earlier, "proud despite years of suffering," as one observer put it. The crutches were gone. He gripped a cane with his right hand and his son Elliott's arm with his left. And again he delivered a speech that provoked at least as much admiration for Roosevelt himself as it did for Governor Smith. "This is a civilized man," a journalist wrote. "For a moment we are lifted up."

This time Smith won his party's nomination easily.

His opponent in the national campaign would be the Republican Herbert Hoover, a much-admired figure who had made a small fortune as an engineer consulting with mining corporations around the world. Then he had supervised the massive effort to help refugees displaced in World War I. He'd gone to Washington as President Coolidge's secretary of commerce. In 1928, he was aiming for the White House—a businessman running for president just when a great many Americans were in thrall to business. Thanks to a great surge in manufacturing fueled by the spread of the automobile and easy credit for consumers, there was a sense in the air that permanent prosperity had arrived at last. Hoover was its herald. He appealed to people who were already comfortable or hoped to be very soon.

Against Hoover, Al Smith was summoning the loyalty of those not included in the great ascendancy of the middle class, especially the masses of Catholic immigrants in the cities who wanted Prohibition overturned. If Smith could bring those new Americans into a coalition with the old Democratic stronghold of the South, he had a shot against Hoover. But even at the start, to anyone in the know, that outcome looked like a long shot.

As the convention closed, FDR was expecting to play a big role in Smith's campaign, perhaps as director of publicity. But he soon realized that Al's top lieutenants meant to use him solely as "window dressing." One of these was Belle Moskowitz, the campaign manager, a brilliant political tactician who brought her knitting to meetings of Smith's inner circle. She had always regarded FDR as a "stuffed shirt"—a pompous phony—and a threat to her boss. Smith's other key aide was Joseph Proskauer, a hard-nosed lawyer and judge who resented FDR for failing to give him credit for writing parts of Roosevelt's big convention speech in 1924. Moskowitz and Proskauer stuck FDR on a couple of committees. When he wanted to talk with Al in person, they shooed him away.

So now, as Smith made one risky decision after another, FDR could only watch from a distance. FDR thought Al should soft-pedal his opposition to Prohibition. Instead, Al played it up. FDR urged Smith to campaign against government by and for the wealthy classes, and to build bridges to "dry" Protestant voters in the South. So what did Smith do? When he had to pick the new national chairman of the Democratic Party, he chose his friend John J. Raskob, a corporate executive who was (a) one of the richest men in America, (b) a conservative Catholic who was a friend of the pope, and (c) even "wetter" than Al.

"A number of southern states are in open revolt" against Smith, FDR wrote Van Lear Black. "Frankly, the campaign is working out in a way which I, personally, would not have followed and Smith is burning his bridges behind him. It is a situation in which you and I can find little room for very active work."

FDR couldn't help but see a personal advantage. Day by day, it seemed ever more likely that Smith was going to lose, probably in a landslide. He would no longer be governor of New York, and he would never again be nominated for president. That meant that when Democrats looked for presidential nominees in later years, Al Smith would be out of the running.

"We shall be in a more advantageous position in the long run," FDR hinted to Black.

All he had to do was steer clear of the wreckage. Not long before, he had thought 1928 might be the right year for him to run for governor of New York. Now he was determined to stay out of that race.

———— • ————

As August turned to September and the national campaign moved into full swing, Democratic chieftains across the state of New York were giving Al the same urgent advice: He had to do whatever it took to get Franklin Roosevelt to run for governor.

Smith had ruled Albany for eight of the last ten years. That had meant good things for Democrats. It wasn't just that Democratic policies could be enacted, though that was important. A governor also appoints many people to jobs in state government and has a big say in the awarding of contracts to companies that do projects for the state, from building roads to cleaning state parks. If a Republican came in, those political appointees would be out of work, and the contracts would go to other companies.

So who would follow Al as governor—another Democrat, who would preserve the party's power statewide? Or a Republican, who would cut short the Democrats' glory days?

The Republicans were putting up a strong candidate, Albert Ottinger, the state's attorney general. For the Democrats, it was bad enough that Ottinger was effective and popular. What really scared them was his religion. He was Jewish. In New York, a Jewish Republican with a solid record was the Democrats' worst nightmare.

This was the reason:

In the 1920s, the population of New York State—10.3 million—was split fairly evenly between New York City (5.6 million) and the rest of the state (4.7 million). The city voted for Democrats by lopsided margins. Upstate—the vast region from the city's northern suburbs all the way west to the Great Lakes—was Republican territory, apart from a few urban enclaves.

Upstate, a great many people were Protestants who favored Prohibition and didn't care for Al Smith, the Tammany man with his flashy suits and low manners. They tended to vote Republican.

Downstate, many voters were Jewish liberals. Early in Al Smith's career, many of those voters had distrusted him because of his connections to the

Tammany machine. But they had since come to trust him as a true progressive who looked out for their interests. Most voted Democratic. But in Albert Ottinger they were being offered the first Jewish candidate ever nominated for statewide office in New York. Even Jewish voters accustomed to voting for Smith would be tempted to switch to Ottinger.

Anyone could do the math. If the Republicans could add any sizable number of downstate Jewish voters to their traditional majorities upstate, they had a winner in Albert Ottinger.

Could any candidate beat him?

No Democrat based in New York City enjoyed anything like Al's popularity. Smith had been *too* popular. In his shadow it had been hard for any younger politician in the city to make a sizable reputation.

Upstate, on the other hand, Democrats spied one figure who could mount a strong threat to Attorney General Ottinger.

He was a Democrat, of course. He spent much of his time—when he wasn't in Georgia—at home in Manhattan. But in politics, he was identified with his ancestral home in the Hudson Valley, with its air of country estates and "good breeding." He had none of the low-class reputation that upstaters associated with Tammany Hall. He was against Prohibition, but he seldom talked about it. And he carried the same last name as the greatest Republican since Lincoln.

Democrats could do their own math. With FDR as their candidate for governor, they could fight for a respectable share of upstate Republicans still loyal to the name Roosevelt. As a well-known progressive, FDR could compete for Jewish votes in the city. Add Smith loyalists downstate who would favor the Democratic nominee no matter what, and he'd be in the running against Ottinger.

But what about infantile paralysis?

Well, the leaders of New York's Democratic strongholds from Brooklyn to Buffalo had just watched FDR walk across that stage at the Houston convention—with help, yes, but he looked so much stronger than he had four years earlier. And hadn't they been reading newspaper stories about his inspiring recovery? As his admirers were saying, you didn't have to be an acrobat to be governor of New York. He looked well. He looked ready. They had to pick a nominee for governor at the state convention in Rochester in just a few weeks. Roosevelt was their best shot, probably their only shot. And they said so to Al with increasing urgency every day.

But Al wasn't so sure.

Sure, he would say, he liked Frank (as he called Roosevelt) pretty well. Who didn't? But he just couldn't take him seriously. Being governor of New York was a tough job, too tough for a fancy-pants fellow from the Ivy League. "Smith thinks of Roosevelt as kind of a Boy Scout," said a party veteran. FDR was the sort of man who could make a fine speech but wasn't built for the kind of backroom dealing that real politics required. He "just isn't the kind of man you can take into the pissroom and talk intimately with," Smith told a friend.

And was he really strong enough? The job had worn Smith out, and he was healthy, more or less. How could a "crippled" man handle it?

But the boys in the party kept pushing him. It had to be Roosevelt, they said. He was the only prospect with vote-getting power both upstate and down.

Then, as the last days of August passed away, Smith's need grew more desperate.

Even in New York State, public opinion seemed to be swinging in favor of Herbert Hoover. Nothing could be harder for Smith to hear. New York was not only his political base and the foundation of his chance for the presidency but also the place he loved, the place where he had made good as a kid who'd sold fish to pay his mother's bills. It would be bad enough to lose the presidency to Hoover. But losing the electoral votes of his home state would be a catastrophic blow to Al's pride. He needed every advantage he could find, including the strongest possible Democrat for governor to share the ballot with him.

So Smith got FDR on the phone down in Warm Springs. *What about it?* The party needed him. Would he run?

Absolutely not, FDR said—doctors' orders.

But Al wasn't giving up. He called in Ed Flynn, the young Democratic boss of the Bronx, who was friendly with FDR. *You talk to him*, Smith told Flynn.

Then he set off on a long campaign tour by train, heading west toward towns where a Catholic product of big-city politics had never before presented himself as a nominee for the presidency.

———— ♦ ————

In Warm Springs, FDR had settled in at his new cottage. Eleanor was in New York, knee-deep in the Smith campaign, but Missy was with him, as was Irvin McDuffie, an Atlanta barber FDR had hired to take over as his valet, the "body man" who helped with the everyday tasks of dressing, bathing, and moving by wheelchair in private.

FDR had been thinking about where to station himself at public occasions when he would be chatting with a lot of people. He couldn't very well sit in a chair while talking with someone who was standing. Staying seated while everyone else was standing called attention to his handicap. Standing with canes or crutches was even more conspicuous, and with both his hands occupied, he wouldn't be able to shake hands. He could stand by himself while leaning against a lectern, but that was for giving a speech, not chatting at a reception.

Maybe he could stand with his back against a wall. Could he stay standing without a cane and shake hands over and over? He practiced it, but he kept losing his balance.

Then one of his Warm Springs neighbors, Leighton MacPherson, went up to Roosevelt's screen door one day and called out to see if he was home. He heard FDR call back, inviting him to come inside. MacPherson went into the main room and there was Roosevelt, standing with his braces on, his back to a wall and extending his arms to right and left, like a trapeze walker on a wire.

"Look at me, Leighton," he said. "I'm standing alone."

———◦◆◦———

Obeying Al Smith's orders, Ed Flynn, calling from the Bronx, got FDR on the phone, long-distance.

No dice, Eddie, Roosevelt said. He could not and would not run for governor.

———◦◆◦———

On Sunday mornings in rural Virginia, preachers were instructing their congregations to stand and split up into two groups. Those for righteousness and Herbert Hoover should stand on one side of the room, those for Satan and Al Smith on the other. Tennessee had voted Democratic in thirteen of the last fourteen presidential elections. But in the fall of 1928, throngs of female Tennessee Democrats were attending meetings of pro-Hoover women's clubs. The rising sentiment against Smith drew on fear of immigrants, fear of gangland crime, and fear that as president, Smith would bring about the repeal of Prohibition.

The greatest fear drew on ancient beliefs among some Protestant Americans that the Roman Catholic Church was greedy, corrupt, and sinister. In Methodist and Baptist pulpits throughout the South, ministers were echoing the Ku Klux Klan's warning that if Smith took over the White House, the pope would rule the United States from behind the scenes. In the rural Southwest, enemies of Smith distributed copies of a photograph showing him celebrating the opening of the famous Holland Tunnel, which linked Manhattan to New Jersey. But the caption on the photo said Smith was preparing to extend the tunnel under the Atlantic Ocean to the world headquarters of the Catholic Church in Rome. A western journalist said Democrats in his state who opposed Smith "do not hesitate to say they are against him because he is a Roman Catholic," he said. "You can find men and women, and they are by no means few, who seem to believe that Smith's election would result in civil war."

In the Klan stronghold of Oklahoma, Smith raged against a "spirit of hatred" abroad in the land. John J. Raskob, the new chairman of the Democratic National Committee, insisted that every Catholic American would defend the U.S. Constitution to the death. But their protests did little good among those who believed Smith was the apostle of everything wrong with the country. At the end of September, as his campaign train retreated toward New York, he looked out the window at night and saw giant crosses that Klansmen had set afire.

On Saturday, September 29, 1928, Governor Smith's train rolled into Milwaukee, Wisconsin. In just two days, New York's Democrats would open their convention in Rochester, and one day later, they would have to nominate someone for governor.

Smith called FDR again. He conceded that he might lose New York's electoral votes to Hoover. To keep alive any hope of winning the White House, he needed the strongest possible nominee for governor to share the top of New York's ticket.

They went back and forth. Again FDR told Al he wished he could run, but his legs simply weren't ready.

Finally Al said, "Well, you're the doctor," and hung up.

A follow-up telegram from Warm Springs confirmed FDR's "no," and Louis Howe made sure reporters got copies. "My doctors are very definite in stating that the continued improvement in my condition is dependent on my avoidance of cold climate," FDR wrote, "and on taking exercises here at Warm Springs during the cold Winter months. It probably means getting rid of leg braces during the next two Winters and that would be impossible if I had to remain in Albany. As I am only 46 years of age, I feel that I owe it to my family and myself to give the present constant improvement a chance to continue. I must therefore with great regret confirm my decision not to accept the nomination and I know you will understand."

Smith went into a huddle with his aides. Once again, fingers ran down dog-eared lists of next-best candidates.

How about Herbert Lehman, a New York City banker and Democratic activist who could pay for his own campaign? As a Jew, he would be an especially strong choice to oppose Ottinger.

No, said the upstaters—no one outside the city had ever heard of Lehman.

What about Townsend Scudder, a respected justice of the New York State Supreme Court and Al's personal favorite for the nomination?

No, said the city men—Scudder was out of touch, a poor candidate.

Owen D. Young, the president of General Electric? He would be a long shot, and he didn't want to run.

U.S. Senator Robert Wagner? No, he liked the Senate and wanted to stay there.

It was Roosevelt or disaster.

It's tempting to think FDR was secretly hoping the Democrats would force him to run by nominating him against his stated wishes. Then his campaign would appear to be a noble gesture for the good of the party. But FDR calculated every step with an eye toward the long run. If he ran for governor now and lost, his hopes for the presidency would take a terrible hit. A race for governor in 1928 was just too risky—both he and Howe were convinced of it. In a private note to his mother, FDR wrote: "I have had a difficult time turning down the Governorship—letters and telegrams by the dozen begging me to save the situation by running. But I have been perfectly firm—I only hope they don't try to stampede the Convention—nominate me and then adjourn!"

It wasn't just the idea of losing that was keeping him from running. There was something happening with his legs. We don't know exactly what it was. The only evidence comes to us thirdhand from a friend of Missy LeHand's, Grace Tully, who would become another of FDR's assistants. Many years later, Tully wrote of a conversation she had with Missy about what happened at Warm Springs that weekend. Missy told Tully that while FDR was practicing his walking in the presence of Missy, Dr. Hubbard, and Helena Mahoney, he had taken a few steps on his own across the living room of his cottage—without canes or crutches. If true, that was extraordinary. But it is very hard to believe, given everything we know about the state of FDR's legs in 1928. He just didn't have the strength in his lower body to keep his balance without support. But even if Tully was wrong about the details, the mere fact that Missy told Tully this story suggests that *something* significant happened—something that may have given FDR new hope that he might be able to walk on his own, if only he could give enough time to more exercise.

———————•◆•———————

Monday, October 1, was the day there had to be a decision on the nomination for governor.

In Rochester, Smith and his team arrived by train and went directly into meetings at the Seneca Hotel.

Meanwhile, down in Georgia, FDR sorted through the latest pile of telegrams urging him to accept the nomination. One was one from his daughter: "GO AHEAD AND TAKE IT! MUCH LOVE. ANNA." (He wired back: "YOU OUGHT TO BE SPANKED. MUCH LOVE. PA.")

Missy was against it. She glared at FDR and said: "Don't . . . you . . . dare!"

FDR asked for a car to be brought up to the cottage. At the wheel was Egbert Curtis, the young manager of the Meriwether Inn, a favorite of FDR's whom he called by the nickname Curt. FDR, Missy, and Irvin McDuffie got in. FDR was scheduled to give a speech in Manchester, the next town to the southeast, down State Route 41. He wasn't supposed to speak until evening, but he wanted to get out of Warm Springs early, just to make sure he couldn't be called to the telephone.

———— ◆ ————

At the convention in Rochester, Eleanor was going from meeting to meeting as head of the women's division of the Democratic State Committee. But she was due to catch an evening train back to New York so she could teach the next morning.

Then she saw one of Al Smith's men trying to get her attention.

Would she mind coming up to speak to the governor for a moment?

It's hard to be sure how Eleanor felt about the idea of her husband running for governor. Later she told her son Jimmy that she had not opposed it. She still believed Franklin was overcommitted to Warm Springs, moneywise and timewise, and she thought a race for governor, win or lose, might help pull him away from Georgia. She was deeply committed to Al Smith's campaign for president, and she thought FDR could help Smith win.

But she and FDR had agreed that he would make his own decisions about whether and when he would run for office.

When Smith and his lieutenants brought her in, she said straight off that she would not urge Franklin to take the nomination.

That was fine, they said. What they wanted to know was this: What was the real truth about his health? Would it actually endanger his well-being if he made the race? Was that why he was saying no?

She recalled later: "I had to say I didn't think it would hurt Franklin's health, but Franklin believed that he might go further in his ability to [walk] and therefore he wanted to keep himself free to go on with his Warm Springs treatment."

She was just repeating what FDR had said. But at least Smith now had reason to think a race for governor wouldn't actually cause Roosevelt harm.

Ed Flynn, the Bronx Democratic boss, had been saying he thought FDR was refusing to run because he had to safeguard his investment in Warm Springs. So Smith pulled the multimillionaire John Raskob into the conversation with Eleanor. What if Raskob promised to take over FDR's obligation for Warm Springs? Would that change his mind?

As Eleanor recalled this part of the conversation, she said, "No, I don't think so."

Raskob didn't hear it that way. He thought Eleanor was saying—or implying, at least—that FDR's real reason for not running was financial.

So maybe Raskob could change FDR's mind. He said he could eliminate FDR's worries about paying for Warm Springs with the stroke of a pen.

The hour was getting late. Smith asked Eleanor for one more favor: Would she please call her husband for them? Maybe she could get him to come to the phone. She said she would try.

The governor's people had found out that FDR was in Manchester to give a speech. They placed a call to the local drugstore. The manager of the store sent someone over to find FDR. His wife wanted him on the telephone, they said. So he came over to the store, and when he picked up the phone, Eleanor said Governor Smith wished to speak to him. Then she handed the receiver to Al.

Right away FDR told Smith the phone connection was bad, and he hung up. But the operator called back a minute later and said Governor Smith would phone Mr. Roosevelt at the Meriwether Inn in a few minutes.

On the ride back Missy kept saying: "Don't you *dare*."

At the inn FDR took the call. On the other end he heard Raskob's voice. He was offering to take responsibility for FDR's debt.

Then Smith himself was back on the line, saying FDR could be governor and still spend nine months a year in Georgia if he wanted to.

"Don't hand me that baloney," FDR said. No governor with any self-respect could neglect the job that way.

Well, Smith said, how about if they put Herbert Lehman on the ticket for lieutenant governor? He would make a great backup. He could fill in if FDR needed him.

At one point FDR asked to speak to Eleanor again. Frances Perkins, who was in the room, reported the conversation as follows, based on what she heard Eleanor say and what she learned later that FDR said:

FDR: "Do you think carrying New York [for Smith] depends on my running for governor?"

Eleanor: "I'm afraid it does."

FDR: "It appears that they think I have an obligation to run. What do you think?"

Eleanor: "I know it's hard, but that's what they believe."

Al Smith got back on the line. He put his need as plainly and forcefully as he could.

As a personal favor, he said, would FDR please take the nomination for governor to improve Smith's chances to win the presidency?

To answer once and for all, FDR had to think about several other questions at once.

If he said yes and lost the race for governor—and he thought he probably *would* lose, just as he thought Smith would lose to Herbert Hoover— then his future in politics would look grim indeed. In 1920, when he was the Democratic nominee for vice president, his ticket had lost the state of New York. This would be a second statewide loss. After that, who would want a two-time loser to run for anything?

But if he said no and then Smith lost the White House by a hair, how would his fellow Democrats feel about the man who had said no when Al Smith begged for his help?

But what about his legs?

If he ran for governor and won, would he be sacrificing his last chance at walking? Dr. Hubbard had told him he might regain 20 percent more strength below the waist. Would that be enough to walk without braces?

Maybe, but only if he stuck to his exercises for many more months, which he could never do as governor of New York—certainly not at Warm Springs, the only place where he could make real progress.

If he didn't run, maybe he'd be able to walk.

If he ran, maybe he'd be governor. As governor, he would be in a much better position to run for president.

He still hadn't given Smith an answer. The governor tried his final angle.

If the convention went ahead and nominated FDR on Tuesday without his consent in advance, Smith asked, would he refuse to run?

"Don't . . . you . . . dare!" Missy whispered.

FDR hesitated.

This is what he told his uncle Fred in a letter several days later: "The convention was in a hopeless quandary—there was no one else to satisfy all parts of the State. It was a condition which spelt defeat not only for the State, but also in all probability for the National ticket in New York. That being so there was literally nothing that I could do but to tell the Governor not that I would allow the use of my name before the convention, but that if in the final analysis the convention insisted on nominating me, I should feel under definite obligation to accept the nomination."

That was good enough for Al. He hung up the phone in triumph and told his boys to pass the word: Nominate Roosevelt!

FDR got in the car for the brief ride from the inn back to his cottage.

Behind the wheel was Egbert Curtis. He asked, *So . . . are you going to run?*

"Curt," he said, "when you're in politics, you've got to play the game."

———— ◆ ————

The next day the convention nominated FDR in a storm of applause.

He accepted by telegram.

EVERY PERSONAL AND FAMILY CONSIDERATION HAS BEEN AND IS AGAINST MY BECOMING THE CANDIDATE OF THE CONVENTION, he wrote,

BUT IF BY ACCEPTING I CAN HELP THE SPLENDID CAUSE OF OUR BELOVED GOVERNOR I WILL YIELD TO YOUR JUDGMENT . . . IF ELECTED, I SHALL GIVE MY BEST SERVICE TO THE MAINTENANCE OF THE HIGH EXAMPLE SET DURING ALL THESE YEARS BY GOVERNOR SMITH AND TO THE FUR-THERANCE OF THE CAUSE OF GOOD GOVERNMENT IN THE STATE OF NEW YORK.

He kept a couple of appointments in Georgia. Then, on Friday, October 5, he boarded a northbound train.

The election was thirty-two days away.

Chapter 14

"ON MY FEET"

. . . .

The Democrats of New York had done something no political party had done before. They had chosen a man most people would call a cripple to run for statewide office.

Surely, many Republicans thought, that would give their own nominee a huge advantage.

But it would not be a simple matter to turn Roosevelt's infirmity against him. By the rules of good sportsmanship, it would be bad behavior to strike at a man who was physically vulnerable. A boxer drew a penalty if he hit an opponent who was down on one knee. Boy Scouts were forbidden from hurting "the weak and helpless." Even in the tough game of politics, voters didn't like it if you took a cheap shot at an opponent with a visible weakness.

Albert Ottinger had no taste for exploiting FDR's handicap. He announced he would make no speeches until the last two weeks of the campaign, and when he did speak, he would refrain from any "mudslinging" or "destructive criticism."

So editorial writers for the state's powerful Republican newspapers stepped up to fight on Ottinger's behalf.

Some went right ahead and broke the rules of good sportsmanship, saying FDR was "a sick man . . . in a sanitarium," that he "cannot stand the strain."

But most were more clever. They saw a chance to undermine confidence in FDR by striking at the bigger target of Al Smith himself.

Franklin Roosevelt, the Republican writers said, was the finest of men, "a thorough gentleman," "able and honest." The one who deserved the public's scorn, they said, was not FDR but Al Smith, who had cruelly pressured his friend to sacrifice his health to advance Smith's chances for the White House.

"There is something both pathetic and pitiless in the 'drafting' of Franklin D. Roosevelt by Alfred E. Smith," said the Republican editorial page of the *New York Evening Post*. Even FDR's closest friends should refrain from voting for him, the *Post* argued, since "they will know that not only the 'cold climate' of Albany but also its killing hard work are no curatives for a man struggling out of one of the most relentless of modern diseases."

"Nothing has been more amazing in the career of Gov. Smith," said the *Buffalo News*, "than his display of callousness with respect to his friend's health."

FDR hit back hard and fast. Even before he left Warm Springs for New York, he had a statement dictated to New York reporters by telephone.

"I am amazed to hear that efforts are being made to make it appear that I have been 'sacrificed' by Gov. Smith to further his own election," he said, "and that my personal friends should vote against me to prevent such sacrifice. Let me set this matter straight at once. I was not dragooned into running by the governor . . . I was drafted because all of the party leaders . . . insisted that my often-expressed belief in the policies of Governor Smith made my nomination the best assurance to the voters that these policies would be continued . . . I trust this statement will eliminate this particular bit of nonsense from the campaign from the very beginning."

Smith, too, debunked the charge that he had forced a sick man to do his bidding.

No, he told reporters at the state capital, of course he had not promised Roosevelt that if the Democratic ticket was elected, Herbert Lehman, as lieutenant governor, would do most of the governor's day-to-day work—that was an "absurdity." (In fact, Smith had proposed just that to FDR.)

"The real fact is this," Smith said. "Frank Roosevelt is mentally as good today as he ever was in his life. Physically he is as good as he ever was in his life. His whole problem is in his lack of muscular control of his lower limbs. But the answer to that is a governor does not have to be an acrobat. We do not elect him for his ability to do a double back flip or a handspring. The work of a governor is brain work. Ninety-five percent of it is accomplished sitting at a desk. There is no doubt about his ability to do it."

But just a few hours earlier, aboard his private railroad car, Smith had said something quite different. He'd been riding from Rochester back to Albany with a few pals from Tammany Hall, sharing in the general satisfaction over getting FDR on the ticket. But one of the men, Daniel Finn, an up-and-comer in the Tammany organization, wasn't so sure that nominating Roosevelt would work out well for Smith.

"Al," Finn said, "aren't you afraid you're raising up a rival who will one day cause you trouble?"

According to a Democratic official who got the story from a man who was listening in, Smith replied: "No, Dan—he won't live a year."

That sounds unbelievably cold. It was true that Smith "could be extremely harsh on occasions in private conversation," as a politician who knew him well put it, "and he always said what was on his mind regardless of the effect it had on the other fellow's feelings." But harsh though he might have been, Smith was not a cold man. So maybe that report of what he said got a word or two wrong. Maybe what Smith really said was: "He won't *last* a year," meaning he thought simply that FDR lacked the physical stamina to remain in office for long. If so, Lieutenant Governor Herbert Lehman would succeed to the governorship, a result that Smith probably would have preferred in the first place.

But whether he said "live" or "last," it's clear that Governor Smith had deep doubts about FDR's fitness either to make the campaign or to hold the governorship.

Al's political chieftains—the ones who kept pressing for a draft of FDR—harbored the same doubts. They said he should take the campaign slow and easy, giving just a few major speeches.

Louis Howe was pressing the same advice on his boss. "Insist on limiting speeches to the four big cities with a radio hookup," he urged FDR. And he was all for having Lehman do most of the campaigning. "He wants to relieve you of all routine work as Governor, and it is a grand time to start now."

Howe was still distraught over the nomination, which he had opposed with every argument he could muster. On the morning after FDR signaled his consent to be drafted, Howe was at work at the headquarters of the Democratic National Committee in New York City. A party official named Adolphus Ragan looked up to see Howe coming into his office. Howe held a telegram in his hand. Without a word he handed the slip of paper to Ragan. It was from FDR, giving Howe the news about his decision to run, contrary to all Howe's advice.

Ragan read the telegram, then looked up to see tears on Howe's cheeks.

"Ragan," Howe said, "they are killing the best friend I ever had in the world."

Howe and Al Smith held entirely different views of Roosevelt. Smith still saw FDR as a fancy-pants political amateur. Howe admired and revered him and thought that with more time and physical therapy he could do anything.

But both men looked at FDR and could not believe he was up to the challenges of campaigning and governing. Despite all his progress at Warm Springs, all the improvements in his ability to walk, other people still saw him as a man deeply compromised.

That was how most people who knew him felt. Certainly it was the view of Missy LeHand, who spent more time with FDR than anyone. Strangers got the same impression. The reaction of Missy's friend, Grace Tully, was typical. One day, in an office corridor, she saw Louis Howe walking slowly at the side of a man Tully recognized instantly as FDR. He "was moving on crutches and with the labored gait taught to infantile paralysis cripples at the Warm Springs Foundation. Louie stopped me and presented me to his boss . . . FDR smiled broadly and shook hands. The vitality in his face contrasted sharply with the helplessness of his legs and I couldn't help but feel the tragedy of such a physical misfortune." When Tully was brought onto FDR's staff that fall, she got another shock. "The first time I saw him lifted out of his wheelchair and carried by valet and chauffeur to a place in his automobile, I turned away and cried."

FDR was acutely aware of reactions like Tully's. So now, whether by deliberate calculation or sheer instinct—probably a combination of the two—he set out to assert control over how he appeared to a vast public of ten million strangers.

———— ◆ ————

Three weeks was only enough time for one long loop of the state. He would start with a westward trek across New York's "lower tier" counties all the way out to Jamestown, just short of the Pennsylvania line; then north to Buffalo; then back east through Rochester and Syracuse to Albany; then down to New York City for the last few days before Election Day.

He started out on the morning of Wednesday, October 17, 1928, when he boarded the auto ferry that would take him across the Hudson to Hoboken, New Jersey. From there he would ride the Erie Railroad to the upstate town of Binghamton, where he would give his first major speech of the campaign that night.

On the auto ferry that morning FDR was sitting in a passenger seat in his car, chatting about the traffic of ships and boats on the lower Hudson. A few big-league Democrats down from Albany stood around talking with him. One of them was Maurice Bloch, leader of the Democrats in the state assembly, whom the party had installed as FDR's campaign manager. Bloch had told FDR he could restrict his campaigning to a few speeches in the big cities to preserve his strength.

Quite plainly and firmly, FDR had said no to that plan.

His energy and strength were quite all right, he told Bloch and the others. In fact, he intended to make the most vigorous and energetic campaign anyone in the state of New York had ever seen. "There will be a lot of handshaking and close contact with the voters if I have my way," he had promised reporters.

On the ferry that morning was a young lawyer named Samuel Rosenman. He had served five years in the state assembly, then taken a job drafting legislative proposals for the Democrats in Albany. Bloch had assigned him to accompany FDR on the campaign trip; he could bring the candidate up to speed on state issues, do research, and help with speechwriting. Bloch brought him over to meet Roosevelt.

Rosenman had seen FDR only once before, from a distance, at the 1924 convention in Madison Square Garden. Now he saw him up close.

As a member of Smith's circle in Albany, Rosenman remembered later, "I had heard stories of his being something of a playboy and idler, of his weakness and ineffectiveness. That was the kind of man I had expected to meet."

On the Hudson River ferry, he saw someone quite different. "The broad jaw and upthrust chin, the piercing, flashing eyes, the firm hands—they did not fit the description." And the remarks about FDR as a weakling "became a joke within a week after I met him . . . I never saw a man who worked harder."

That was the impression FDR intended to make on the voters of New York. In the recesses of his own mind, he might not have been sure he was ready to take on the physical challenge of the campaign. But he was going to do so, ready or not, and dare anyone who watched him to say he wasn't up to it. And by doing so, he might just banish any doubts of his own.

———— ◆ ————

His first public appearance was supposed to be that night in Binghamton. Instead, whenever the train pulled into a small-town station, he got up from his seat, walked to the platform of the last car, and talked to whoever showed up, starting with the depot at Port Jervis, the first town over the New Jersey line.

He beamed out at the crowd and called, "How do you do, neighbors?" He introduced a couple of people. Then he said, "I think I look pretty healthy for a sick man, don't you?"

He heard appreciative laughter and applause. It was the right touch. In those few words he was acknowledging their curiosity about his condition, pushing away any thought of pity, and taking a crack at the Republican scuttlebutt about him.

In the high school gym in Binghamton that night, he declared: "This was supposed to have been my first speech of the active campaign. That was the intention on the part of everybody until I left Jersey City this morning, and the whole thing was knocked into a cocked hat, first at [Port Jervis] and then at [Middletown], and then at Callicoon, and then at Hancock, and then Neponsit, and then at Susquehanna."

By now the crowd was laughing along with him.

"So this is the *seventh* speech of the campaign."

He had spoken at every one of those small-town whistle-stops. As the train rolled up to a station, it was easy enough to lock his braces, stand up, and walk on Irvin McDuffie's strong arm to the platform at the back of the rear car. There a little crowd would be gathered, notified by the morning paper and word of mouth that the nominee for governor was paying them a visit. In the 1920s, that was big news in a small town. They saw a tall, grinning, broad-shouldered, good-looking man emerge onto the platform and move to the railing to wave and then begin to speak. He was brimming with cheer and enthusiasm, able to stand and even to walk. People who saw him in person tossed out any image they had of Franklin Roosevelt as a pathetic man.

—————◆—————

Westward to Owego . . . Elmira . . . Corning . . .

"As all of you know, I am an upstate man, but I believe that the day has passed when there should be war and disputes of any kind between the great metropolitan district and us farmers of upstate."

He shifted from train to automobile, with a few cars for reporters and the other Democratic candidates trailing behind. Traveling by car was better; he could make more stops. He could bypass the awkward business of shifting from train to car for the short drive to a town square or a school to give a speech. Instead, the car could go straight to the spot where he was to meet people and speak, then take off again. One day he made fourteen speeches.

To give a brief, informal talk in a town square or a public park, he would often just lock his braces and stand in the back of the car, speaking to a crowd without even getting out. Then he would sit back down to shake hands and exchange a few words with each man and woman who came up to say hello.

Hornell . . . Wellsville . . . Olean . . .

"You know, some of my Republican friends around New York are talking about the kind of sympathy the people of the state ought to have for this unfortunate invalid who is running for governor! [Applause] I don't think that any of us need worry about that, and I am mighty glad that the convention in Rochester was good enough and kind enough to draft me for the job!"

A man who couldn't walk on his own might be expected to stay away from crowds. In fact, Roosevelt loved the travel and talk that made up a political campaign. "He enjoyed the freedom and getting out among the people," said Frances Perkins. "He used to . . . describe individuals in the crowd—a woman with a baby, an old fellow, small boys scampering in the throng. He associated them sometimes with the town . . . in which he had seen them. His personal relationship with crowds was on a warm, simple level of a friendly, neighborly exchange of affection."

Campaigning meant private meetings with local mayors, council members, judges, sheriffs. He knew that these people, like the crowds of curious voters, weren't sure what to expect. To put them at ease, he developed subtle ways of pulling their attention away from his legs. FDR's face had always been unusually animated, but now he made the most of that trait. His features were constantly in motion. His eyebrows arched high in surprise or scrunched low in serious attention. One moment he might spread his grin to his ears, then thrust out his lower lip in an actor's puzzled pout. Anyone introduced to him met "a big friendly smile," one observer said, "and the glint of intense interest in his sparkling eyes." There were "little laughs, and goads, and urgings, such as 'Really? Tell me more!' . . . 'Well, what do you know?' . . . 'Same thing's happened to me dozens of times!' . . . 'Oh, that's fascinating!'" Perkins said "the heads of little county and local committees pulled up a seat and whispered their deepest hopes to him." In earlier years he might have turned away from these small fry. But in the campaign of 1928, "he sat and nodded and smiled and said, 'That's fine,' when they reported some small progress."

Person by person, he was changing minds, erasing the stigma. A man inclined to write him off as weak, like Samuel Rosenman, came away with an impression of vigor. A woman who first saw him through tears of pathos, like Grace Tully, came away inspired. Among those who saw him every day—his aides and the reporters following the campaign—he was so casual about his legs that after a while they simply forgot he was disabled, as he had seemed to forget it himself.

Jamestown . . . Dunkirk . . . Buffalo . . .

"We have had six outdoor meetings today. I hope you will forgive me if my voice is a little frayed tonight. That is the only part of me, except a couple of weak knees—physically, not morally!"

On October 22, five days out from New York, the campaign came to Rochester, the scene of his nomination. Here he would discuss his disability with more than a passing laugh line.

There was discussion about just how to do this. It was delicate. If he referred to his condition every day, there would be hell to pay. He'd be seen as playing for votes on the basis of pity. He might seem to be preoccupied with his own troubles—hardly what people wanted to see in their governor. "There was an implicit limit on how much [able-bodied people] wanted to hear about our successes and failings," wrote one survivor of polio. "Gradually the lesson was learned that no one including myself really wanted to hear the mundane details of being sick or handicapped, not the triumphs or the hardships."

Still, the question of FDR's strength, as the *New York Times* noted, was "the greatest under-cover issue of his campaign." He wanted to put it out on the table.

He could do so just once, he decided, but no more.

So what should he say?

In the papers of Roosevelt's 1928 campaign there is a single sheet of paper containing some drafted remarks about his disability. It was more than he'd said so far, but not much. It was framed as another jibe at the Republican charges that he'd been "dragooned" to run, and as a rebuttal to the scuttlebutt about his poor health. The draft remarks repeated that he hadn't been "dragooned," that his health was excellent, and that a governor's work was not physical. "Let me assure them [Republican critics] that my only physical disability, which is a certain clumsiness in locomotion and which I trust will eventually disappear, has interfered in no way with my power to think. Possibly because I find it more convenient to sit at my desk than to move around, I pride myself that during the past four years, I have done rather more than the average man's daily stint [of thinking]."

It wasn't quite the right note, and somebody realized it, probably FDR himself. The note *not used* is scribbled in pencil across the top of the sheet.

He and Sam Rosenman traded drafts back and forth, developing something new.

At a reception at Rochester's Seneca Hotel, FDR shook hands with more than eight hundred people. The big event at the city's Convention Hall was scheduled for unusually late in the evening, since people wanted to hear Herbert Hoover give a scheduled address by radio. By the time FDR was driven over to the hall through the October evening, passing sidewalks crammed with onlookers, there were four thousand people in the seats.

As other Democrats made opening remarks, they saw his big-shouldered figure move across the stage in his slow, swaying gait, smiling all the way, then drop into a big armchair. Those watching closely noticed that he reached to one knee, then the other, to unlock his braces so he could bend his legs. When his moment to speak came, he relocked his braces, stood up (with a quick bit of help from an aide), and walked slowly to the lectern. Then he thrust his chin toward the upper gallery and smiled.

"I have been trying to focus in these great night meetings on one topic at a time," he began, "especially because nowadays one talks not just to the fine audience in front of one but also to thousands of people scattered all over the state who are listening in by radio."

Tonight, the topic would be "what I call the human being function of our state government." He promised to build upon the great increase in state spending on education under Governor Smith and to raise standards for teachers.

Then there was the matter of children's health. Infant mortality in New

York had declined under Smith, "but we have only just begun the task, for much remains to be done."

This brought him by quiet steps to his main subject.

"I may be pardoned," he said, "if I refer to my own intense interest in the care of crippled children and, indeed, of cripples of every kind." Not only polio but tuberculosis, industrial accidents, and other misfortunes had disabled some one hundred thousand New Yorkers, children and adults, he said. For practical reasons alone, more must be done to restore these people to productive lives, since "a wheelchair cripple is not only a dead load on the earning power of the community, but in most cases requires also the attention and care of some able-bodied person as well."

Then there was "the great humanitarian side of the subject." As governor, Al Smith had proposed more aid for disabled people, but the Republicans in Albany had shot him down. Why, the state didn't even know how many crippled children there really were—a public nurse had told him so.

"We need an expansion of medical service to every out-of-the-way corner in the cities and on the farms."

Then he got to it.

"I suppose that people readily will recognize that I myself furnish a perfectly good example of what can be done by the right kind of care."

Applause began to rustle through the hall.

"I dislike to use this personal example, but it happens to fit. Seven years ago . . . I came down with infantile paralysis . . . and I was completely—for the moment—put out of any useful activities."

People were rising to clap and cheer. Tears were welling.

"By personal good fortune I was able to get the very best kind of care, and the result of having the right kind of care is that today I am on my feet."

By then it was hard to hear him.

"And while I won't vouch for the mental side of it, I am quite certain that from the physical point of view, I am quite capable of going to Albany and staying there two years!"

It was a clever twist of the topic, even a brilliant one. He had turned his own personal disaster into a plea for humanitarian government. He had defied the whispered rumors. He had turned himself from a man to pity into a man to cheer.

It was a long speech full of proposals, but he ended on a simple note.

He said he detected a surge in the state for "government by common sense and not by statistics." (This was a dig at Herbert Hoover, known as the Great Engineer, a politician inclined to reduce human problems to columns of figures.) "The people want the national government run by a human being and not a machine. Yes, that is a perfectly natural difference. You and I and Al Smith—human beings.

"And so, my friends, as I was coming over this afternoon from Batavia, I thought of a little verse that was taught to me when I was pretty small, and I thought it was a pretty good motto for me in this campaign, a motto that will apply to what we are trying to do in this state . . . and it is this: 'Look outward and not in; look forward and not back; look upward and not down; and lend a hand."

———————— ◆ ————————

Seneca Falls . . . Syracuse . . . Watertown . . . Rome . . . Utica . . . Herkimer . . . Albany . . .

The Roosevelt caravan turned south on Route 9 and headed down through the Hudson Valley toward New York City, where religious loyalties were fueling ugly charges on both sides of the campaign. The powerful publisher William Randolph Hearst, still a sworn enemy of Al Smith and no friend of FDR, charged that Roosevelt had been "trying to drag a religious question into politics" by defending Smith against anti-Catholic attacks. Samuel Untermyer, a prominent Jewish Democrat, praised Herbert Lehman, FDR's running mate, as "a better Jew" than Attorney General Ottinger. But it appeared that the mudslinging over religion might actually be bringing votes to FDR.

A reporter for the *New York Sun* saw evidence that "independent Democrats who are against Smith because he is a Catholic are for Roosevelt. Independent Republicans who are against Ottinger because he is a Jew are for Roosevelt. Ottinger does not seem to be able to profit in this strange division along the lines of intolerance."

In the city the press swarmed around the campaign. There were many newspapers in and around the great city, and some competed for customers by running big photographs to catch the eyes of commuters dashing for the subway. They also kept a sharp eye out for what were called sob stories—articles that catered to the public's enjoyment of sentimentalizing over the fate of people less fortunate than themselves.

These practices in the press posed a new risk. FDR and Howe knew that from certain angles at certain vulnerable moments, the candidate's body in motion could appear, as he had said himself, "clumsy," or worse, difficult to look at. There was a comparable risk in print: Stories of his fight against polio could be told to provoke the maximum output of readers' pity. In both cases, attention would be attracted to FDR's legs.

For all of Howe's tricks in orchestrating press coverage, neither he nor FDR could control it entirely. But they did what they could.

When reporters asked about polio, he would answer, but mostly by describing the programs he had developed at Warm Springs. "I don't want any sob stuff in the relation of my own experience," he would say.

He and Howe worried more about photos and newsreel footage of FDR getting in or out of an automobile. Worst of all would be a chance film clip that showed him taking a fall. At least once he gave newsreel camera operators an explicit directive: "No movies of me getting out of the machine [automobile], boys." In that particular case, an observer said, "the motion picture machines and cameras were turned away until he had gotten out of his car and taken a pose before the photographic apparatus." Whether he asked or not, newspapers generally did not publish photos highlighting his disability.

Such pleas to the press—and the journalists' own reluctance to put the spotlight on a disability in a man they liked and admired—helped to muffle the glaring fact that he could walk in only a very limited way, and that there were many times each day when other people had to lift him, lower him, and carry him. As a man now living much of each day in public, however carefully he calculated his movements, he could not escape the fact that *some* people were going to witness just how dependent he was on others.

So along with all his efforts to persuade people that a "crippled" man could be governor, for all his vigor on the campaign trail and the ingenious tactics he used to divert people's attention away from his legs, he needed to do one last thing, perhaps the hardest of all. In certain situations there was simply no way to deflect attention from his legs, so he had to summon the courage to endure the stares.

Frances Perkins saw this quality in him on the evening of October 31 in the Yorkville neighborhood of Manhattan's Upper East Side. FDR was scheduled to speak in a ballroom at a big community center called the Yorkville Casino. The main doors stood at the top of a broad stone staircase leading up from the sidewalk. There was no railing, which made it impossible for him to climb the stairs on his own. Inside the ballroom, hundreds of milling people were waiting—another obstacle course. The only alternative was to go up the fire escape at the rear of the building, which led to the back of the ballroom. Jimmy Roosevelt and another man linked hands to make a seat for FDR. He lowered himself into that seat and put his arms around the men's shoulders. Then the men slowly and carefully carried him up the stairs.

In the ballroom, some fifty people were waiting to join FDR on the speaker's platform. Some of them watched as he was carried up the fire escape, Perkins among them.

"Those of us who saw this incident," she wrote later, "with our hands on our throats to hold down our emotion, realized that this man had accepted the ultimate humility which comes from being helped physically. He had accepted it smiling. He came up over that perilous, uncomfortable, and humiliating 'entrance,' and his manner was pleasant, courteous, enthusiastic. He got up on his braces, adjusted them, straightened himself, smoothed his hair, linked his arm in his son Jim's, and walked out on the platform as if this were nothing unusual."

Sometimes a staircase or a fire escape wasn't wide enough for FDR and two other men. So if he absolutely had to, he could get up and down stairs by himself, as long as there was a strong railing. Anna saw him perform this feat at Flushing High School in Queens. He didn't want to walk up the long center aisle of the auditorium, Anna recalled, "for fear people might think he was trying to develop sympathy for himself—a sympathy aimed at making people vote for a physically courageous man rather than for one with the political and statesmanlike qualities necessary for the office." So here, too, he chose to come in by a fire escape at the rear of the building, one that was apparently too narrow for assistants to carry him. "By using his strong arms and shoulders," Anna wrote, "he could, slowly but surely, swing first one leg and then the other up one step at a time. It was a tough, slow climb, and Father paused for breath a couple of times. Each time he made a wisecrack to break the tension for those of us who were watching. We weren't worried that he might fall. But we knew how he hated to have people watch him doing something that was as much effort as this and that drew attention to his paralysis. When he reached the top, his face was streaming with perspiration, and his white shirt was soaked. He paused just long enough to mop his face and catch his breath. Then he walked out on to the stage . . ."

Watching FDR at one event after another that week, Perkins recalled, "I began to see what the great teachers of religion meant when they said that humility is the greatest of virtues, and that if you can't learn it, God will teach it to you by humiliation. Only so can a man be really great."

———————— ◆ ————————

Every day, Roosevelt told the crowds that he and Al Smith were on the verge of historic upset victories. But by now it was clear to any realistic onlooker that Smith was about to be buried in a landslide.

If his campaign had accomplished nothing else, at least it had persuaded the press that his disability was no handicap. "It is a fact," wrote a *New York World* reporter, "that Mr. Roosevelt appears in better health today than he did at the outset of his campaign three weeks ago."

But toxic rumors continued to circulate. He would be dead within six months. Or if he won and survived, he would soon turn over the governor's chair to Herbert Lehman.

"I thought that with Halloween over these ghost stories would be forgotten," he told listeners at one stop. "All I can say is that if I could keep on in this campaign steadily for another twelve months I would throw away my cane."

In the final days he rushed north for meetings and rallies on his home ground. He spent the day before the election in Poughkeepsie and Hyde Park, slept in his own bed that night, voted in the morning, and then joined Smith in New York City to await the results.

At the Biltmore Hotel, he and Eleanor hosted a buffet supper for friends and allies. He went over to see the Democratic faithful at Tammany headquarters, looked in on the party's national offices at the General Motors Building, then went back to the Biltmore for the long night of waiting.

Early reports from upstate voting precincts were crushing. Ottinger was racing out to a big lead. By midnight the totals showed that Smith had lost his race against Hoover in all but eight states. His beloved New York State had gone against him.

Sam Rosenman watched Roosevelt as he leafed through the county-by-county voting returns. He saw FDR's jaw get set and stony.

"We'll stay around until it is over," he said.

He suspected Republican county sheriffs were delaying their vote reports and doctoring the totals. He had phone calls put through to several of them.

"This is Franklin Roosevelt," he said. "The returns from your county are coming in mighty slowly, and I don't like it . . . I want you personally to see that the ballots are not tampered with."

Finally he concluded there was no point in staying any longer. Now only Frances Perkins and Sara Roosevelt were left to wait for the party workers to hand over the final tally. "I made up my mind to sit out the night on the ridiculous theory that if I didn't give up somehow the result would be changed," Perkins said.

Precinct by precinct, local totals continued to stream in by teletype. The first editions of the newspapers arrived with headlines announcing Hoover's and Ottinger's victories. Still more reports arrived.

At 4:00 A.M., the men tallying the returns came over to tell Sara and Frances Perkins that FDR had been elected governor by twenty-five thousand votes out of nearly 4.5 million cast.

The two women embraced. Then Frances Perkins escorted Sara home to East Sixty-Fifth Street just as the sun was coming up.

"HE MUST DO IT HIMSELF"

·······························

Two years later, on November 4, 1930, Franklin Roosevelt was elected to a second term as governor of New York by the greatest margin of victory ever recorded in the state. This time, against the Republican Charles H. Tuttle, the U.S. attorney for the Southern District of New York, he piled up mountains of votes throughout the city; he won in the upstate cities of Buffalo, Rochester, Syracuse, and Albany; he won in rural counties where farmers had been voting the straight Republican ticket since the days of Abraham Lincoln; he won among Protestants, Catholics, and Jews. He won by nearly three-quarters of a million votes out of roughly three million cast.

The day after the election, at the Biltmore Hotel in New York, one of the governor's lieutenants came out of Democratic Party headquarters to talk with reporters.

This was Big Jim Farley, a friendly Irish American political pro who had moved over from Al Smith's camp to work for FDR. He and Louis Howe had written a statement for the press. They wrote it on their own that morning. FDR had left early for Albany.

Farley read the statement slowly so the reporters could get it down word for word.

"I fully expect," he said, "that the call will come to Governor Roosevelt when the first presidential primary is held, which will be late next year. The Democrats in the nation naturally want as their candidate for president the man who has shown himself capable of carrying the most important state in the country by a record-breaking majority. I do not see how Mr. Roosevelt can escape becoming the next presidential nominee of his party, even if no one should raise a finger to bring it about."

The reporters ran for the telephones.

Farley said later that he and FDR had never discussed a campaign for president before that day. This was a political superstition: You avoided such talk before the time was right.

When Farley figured his boss had reached his office up in Albany, he called him to report what he had said to the press, not sure what the response might be.

FDR just laughed.

"Whatever you said, Jim, is all right with me."

Before the month was out, Louis Howe had rented a new office as a base for a national campaign. And Ed Flynn—the party boss of the Bronx who had urged FDR to run for governor, now Roosevelt's secretary of state, whom FDR believed to be the smartest political organizer in America—was invited up to the governor's residence for the weekend.

Flynn found himself in the governor's private quarters facing only Howe and FDR.

"Eddie," the governor said, "my reason for asking you to stay overnight is that I believe I can be nominated for the Presidency in 1932."

In 1928, when Herbert Hoover won the White House in a landslide, no one would have bet much on a Democrat's chances in 1932. FDR had set his sights on the election year after that, 1936. But in just two years the political landscape had been plowed up as if by a string of tornadoes. The next Democratic nomination was looking much more valuable than anyone had expected.

Roosevelt's crushing majority in 1930 had been bolstered by voters who blamed Republicans for a stock market crash in the fall of 1929 and the economic recession it had triggered—a recession so deep that by the fall of 1930 some people were calling it a depression—a frightening mixture of falling prices and production that puts many people out of their jobs, dries up the credit that businesses need to expand, and threatens to last much longer than the downward loop of the normal business cycle.

But it wasn't just the struggling economy that had given FDR his landslide. New York Democrats running for Congress in 1930 hadn't won by nearly such large margins.

It was what he had done in his short time as governor—not so much the laws he had passed, since the Republicans in the state legislature blocked most of his initiatives, but the powerful impression he had made. Even to people who had seen him as no more than a pale shadow of his Rough Rider cousin, a rich boy dabbling in politics, it was clear that "a new Roosevelt" had come fully and forcefully onto the political scene.

This had happened in stages.

First, he had dealt with the problem of Al Smith.

Smith had been devastated by the loss of both his race for the presidency and his hold on power in New York State. In the wake of the Hoover landslide, he declared that he was out of politics for good, at least as a candidate for high office.

But Al's appetite for influence remained strong. As he watched the man he had practically begged to run for governor prepare to take his place in

Albany, he began to ruminate on all the reasons he had harbored doubts about FDR.

So Smith began to think of himself as a kind of powerful coach—on the sidelines, yes, but calling the plays for an inexperienced and spindly freshman quarterback.

He soon learned that the new quarterback intended to call his own plays.

Even before FDR took the oath of office, Al made his bid to be the power behind the throne.

"Well, Frank," he said, "you won't have to worry about being governor. You can come to Albany for the inauguration and stay around for a while and get the hang of things, and when you get a chance you can hop back to Warm Springs, and we'll be here to see that things go all right."

"Al," FDR replied, "did you ever leave Albany for an extended stay during a legislative session?"

"No," Smith conceded.

"Then I won't either," FDR said.

Then Smith urged FDR to reappoint two of his own most trusted aides, especially Belle Moskowitz, whose title was secretary but who in fact was Smith's most powerful behind-the-scenes operator and his most devoted loyalist.

No, the new governor said politely, he needed his own people close to him.

When FDR told Frances Perkins about this exchange, she was struck by his determination to make his own decisions, tempting as it might be to make concessions to Smith just to keep the peace. She had a "very real sense, as I rode home on the train that night, of this man, sick and struggling . . . just grabbing to keep his will power. He must do it himself. He must think it himself . . . It must be his."

Early in 1929, FDR invited Smith to stay overnight at the governor's residence for a couple of weekends. But the Saturday dinner table was crowded with guests, and FDR went up to bed before Al could take him aside to talk. In the morning, Smith attended mass while FDR slept in. More guests came in and out all afternoon, and then Smith had to catch the train for New York. For a while, Perkins said, Al "didn't realize he was getting the brush-off."

Finally he did get it, and he began to get angry.

He had made FDR governor, he would say, and now he got only ingratitude and the cold shoulder?

FDR wondered who owed whom. Hadn't he done what Al wanted? Hadn't he given up his last chance of walking when Al said he needed Roosevelt's help?

He had no intention of being anything but his own man as governor. He was in. Al was out. That was it.

It worked—for the moment. People in Albany saw that Al was indeed out.

But the former governor nourished a simmering anger.

———— ◆ ————

As a private citizen, FDR had been managing his affairs without much one-on-one contact with strangers. But a governor can't conduct business from a back office with a couple of aides—not if he wants to get big things done.

So FDR developed routines for being a public man who couldn't walk on his own.

Since 1921 he had learned a lot about managing his movements in public and making people feel comfortable in his presence. Now, in the endless flow of meetings and receptions, he raised that ability to a high art form.

He made no attempt to hide himself away in inner offices. Quite the contrary: He made himself available to practically everybody. "There is no disguising the fact . . . that he is a crippled man," reported Milton MacKaye, a writer for the *New Yorker* magazine, who spent time watching Roosevelt at work, "and one of the admirable things about Roosevelt is that he never attempts to disguise it. Getting in to see the Governor is hardly more difficult than dropping in on your pastor. He will see anyone, and by anyone I mean that even insurance salesmen have eluded his secretaries."

Mobility was a little easier now, since as governor he could hire more help. Irvin McDuffie stayed on as his personal valet, helping especially with morning and evening routines. He was joined by two state policemen, Gus Gennerich and Earl Miller, who acted not only as bodyguards but as physical helpers. These three plus the man FDR appointed as his official secretary, Guernsey Cross, a former All-American basketball player at Cornell University, gave FDR round-the-clock help getting where he needed to go. Any of them—in pairs or even alone, if necessary—could carry FDR quickly up or down steps and stairs, and each became proficient at managing FDR's wheelchair.

Since 1921, Roosevelt had relied on his plain wooden wheelchairs to move around inside whatever home or office he happened to be using, whether at East Sixty-Fifth Street, Hyde Park, or Warm Springs. He put on his braces and stood up to walk only when he felt he had to—typically at public appearances where he wanted to display the extent of his physical recovery.

In other words, walking was essentially for show.

In private there was no need to walk, so the wheelchair was brought out. It made everything easier and quicker. If new employees were uneasy at first sight of the governor in a wheelchair, they soon became just as used to it as they were to his long cigarette holder. "The first physical thing that struck you on meeting Roosevelt was that huge, powerful body without the use of legs," Sam Rosenman recalled later. "As you got to know Roosevelt, it was also the first thing you forgot. The wheelchair, always present in the background, soon became a normal part of the furniture of the room. Wheeling him in to dinner or to bed became as routine as offering your arm to your dinner partner. It was something that he himself seemed never to think about much. In fact, when he wanted to end a conversation or a visit, he frequently would say: 'Well, I'm sorry, I have to run now!'—and I'm sure it never struck him as a strange thing to say."

For people outside his inner circle, he developed different habits.

He preferred to be seen in the wheelchair as little as possible by people who didn't know him well. He had to talk with them—dozens of them every week—easily and confidentially. So the wheelchair was used, but used carefully.

When a meeting was about to occur, one of FDR's attendants would make sure the governor was already seated in a regular chair and ready to welcome his guest. Meanwhile the wheelchair was put away until it was needed next.

When Al Smith had said a governor didn't need to be an acrobat, he hadn't known much about wheelchairs. Moving from a wheelchair to a regular chair or back again—an action FDR performed several times each day—was something of an athletic feat, and his attendant had to be agile, too. Only a few knew how to help—the bodyguards, McDuffie, and the Roosevelts' sons.

When FDR was ready to get into the wheelchair, his helper would hold the chair at a right angle to where he was seated, making sure to hold it rock-steady with both hands and a knee to brace one wheel. Then FDR would push hard on the arms of his regular chair, thrust upward, twist his body in midair, and land on the seat of the wheelchair. The family called this "the flip." There was always a danger that the chair would slip or that FDR would lean too far to one side or the other. He didn't wind up on the floor often, but it happened. The family always watched the move with a little twinge of nerves. This, too, was a reason he couldn't use the wheelchair in front of strangers. The risk of an embarrassing fall was too great. So, as often as possible, "the flip" was done behind closed doors. When he was back in a regular chair, the doors were opened, and the guests found a busy executive ready to greet them. He just shook their hands without standing up.

Often the governor would host receptions where important business was done in casual snatches of conversation. A governor who was able to walk on his own could move around the room, chatting for a moment with this member of the state assembly or that Democratic donor, fitting in dozens of quick exchanges in an evening. He could also evade a windbag who wouldn't shut up. None of this was possible for FDR, who was stuck in one place for the duration of the reception.

So Eleanor and Frances Perkins—who was now FDR's top-ranking labor official—devised a system for accomplishing the same ends. They would recruit a few friends to act as scouts, then post the scouts in the crowd with special instructions about who the governor did and didn't care to speak with. If a scout spotted an unwelcome guest homing in on FDR, she would intercede and start a conversation with that person. If another guest was taking too much of the governor's time, Eleanor would send a scout to find someone FDR *did* want to speak with and ask: "Wouldn't you like to have a little talk with the governor?" Over they would come, sending the too-talkative guest on their way.

———————◆———————

There was a danger that the broad voting public would imagine him as a lonely man trapped in an office by his lifeless legs. He prevented any such problem by stepping right into voters' kitchens and parlors through the still-novel medium of radio. FDR knew very well that one of his best tools was his voice, and he used it to splendid effect in an occasional series of informal radio talks about issues pending in Albany. In a warm, casual tone so unlike the speech of most politicians, he talked about complicated problems of government in a way that anybody could understand. The talks by radio would come to be called FDR's "fireside chats." No tactic did more to make FDR popular.

He devised another means of showing himself to the public as a man in motion.

In decades long past, the state of New York had built an intricate network of canals linking cities and towns from the Hudson River in the east to the St. Lawrence River in the north to the Great Lakes at the state's western end. The grand old Erie Canal was only the most famous of these waterways. In all there were hundreds of miles of canals, most of them still navigable and still used to move freight and passengers, despite the coming of trains and automobiles.

On July 6, 1929, at the town of Waterford, where the Erie joins the Hudson River, FDR with Eleanor and a couple of sons and aides boarded a houseboat-barge and set off on a two-week passage by water to the Niagara country. People in tiny towns where no governor had set foot for a century now shook hands with Franklin Roosevelt down at the canal.

He used the tour to praise the canal system and inspect state facilities along the way—often sending Eleanor to see the innards of prisons, hospitals, and schools—but he was also offering himself for inspection. Just as in the 1928 campaign, people discovered not the "crippled" man they had heard about but a man on the move, passing through their town by the good old method of the canal boat. It was something to see, fun and unusual.

And it reinforced a point. Republicans upstate were already spreading a rumor that Roosevelt was too weak to run for a second term as governor in 1930. In fact, reported the *New York Times* soon after the canal tour, "Mr. Roosevelt, except for his lameness, never has been in better general health. He has had no physical difficulty in performing the duties of Governor. This, it was said, was shown by his recent inspection of the barge canal and state institutions, during which he . . . showed endurance which was not surpassed by any other member of his party."

It had come off so well that he made a tour by canal the next summer, too.

————— ◆ —————

There were times when it was simply impossible to divert the attention of strangers away from his disability.

Early in 1929, a teenager named Philip Hamburger happened to see the new governor give a talk at a small community hall in Manhattan. Eleanor was there with FDR, who sat at a desk as he spoke. There was only one way out of the hall—down a narrow aisle at the side. Many years later, Hamburger, who became a writer, described what he remembered of Roosevelt's departure from the hall: "The distance from desk to street could not have been more than a hundred feet, but it took the Governor an agonizingly long time to traverse it. His legs were in heavy braces . . . The audience, as though hypnotized, did not leave. It stood and watched the Roosevelts depart . . . The Governor was intent upon the task before him: to reach the street and the sanctuary of his limousine . . . Occasionally she leaned over to whisper something in his ear, and he smiled and put the other foot forward. The slow procession became extremely impressive. Mrs. Roosevelt seemed to sense that we knew we should not stay but that we could not leave. Moving slowly along, she thanked many of us for coming . . . Finally the Roosevelts reached the street. The audience, still hypnotized, followed them outside. Mrs. Roosevelt and a chauffeur helped the Governor into his car. His put his head back against the cushions with the expression of a man who has accomplished his mission. Mrs. Roosevelt opened a window of the car and waved . . . An audience of strangers had become friends."

———————— ◆ ————————

His record after two years as chief executive of the nation's biggest state was progressive—probably the most progressive of any among the main candidates for president in 1932. He pushed for shorter hours, higher wages, and better working conditions for laboring people. He championed the causes of pensions for the elderly and more money for education. He helped farmers. He made moves to reform the use of the state's great water resources. He shook up old habits for choosing a governor's assistants. He appointed a fair number of Democratic politicos to state jobs, but he also appointed progressive activists, labor leaders, college professors, and social workers. When the stock market crashed and the economy plunged, he argued that state government should mount compassionate efforts to help the swelling crowds of New Yorkers who had been turned out of their jobs through no fault of their own.

So if Big Jim Farley had exaggerated when he said no one but FDR could possibly be the Democrats' nominee for president in 1932, he was surely right that FDR was the man for other Democrats to beat.

But it was still too early to say out loud what Farley and others close to FDR were sensing—that there was some intangible spark in this man, a promise of something great. Only years later did Farley try to put the feeling into words.

"He was one of the most alive men I had ever met," Big Jim would write. "He never gave me the impression that he was tired or bored . . . He was quick, alert, keen . . .

"I had an intuition that there was a touch of destiny about the man, that he was intended to play a big role in the affairs of his fellow countrymen."

Chapter 16

WHISPERS AND SHOUTS

For a while Americans figured the country was going through nothing much worse than the kind of economic slump that often followed boom times. In May 1930, President Hoover declared: "I am convinced we have passed the worst and with continued effort we shall rapidly recover." There was no need for more federal action, he said, since "the Depression is over."

But all that summer, the season for putting up new buildings, construction workers were losing their jobs. Steel mills and car factories cut production. In the fall, banks here and there began to fail. They could give out no more loans, the lifeblood that businesses needed to grow, and no more mortgages for people buying houses. People who had put their savings into those banks simply lost their money. And fears began to rise that the same might soon happen to many more banks.

The country looked to the White House for help. Hoover made a few cautious moves. He urged business to do better. He blamed Europeans. But he would not stand for the idea of using federal funds to help people in need. He hated speaking in public, and on the radio he sounded like a nervous old crab. The man who had once been a hero, rescuing war refugees and flood victims, now seemed timid, even frightened.

Shortly before FDR's campaign for reelection as governor began in 1930, all delegates to the last Democratic National Convention received a printed newsletter, unsigned, in their mail. A copy landed on the desk of Jim Mahoney, an aide to FDR, who passed it along with a note to Louis Howe. The note read: "Honestly, I could murder for much less."

The newsletter contained an outrageous lie. It said that FDR had been hiding the truth about his paralysis. It was not the result of poliomyelitis, the letter said. It was the result of syphilis, a dreaded bacterial disease usually spread by sexual intercourse. In FDR, as in some other people with syphilis, the bacteria had invaded the spinal cord, causing the person to walk with a jerky, spastic gait. But "the most disgusting, vicious and really dangerous thing about this matter," the piece went on, "is the fact that Governor Roosevelt (with his loathsome and infectious venereal disease) bathes in the same pool with . . . poor innocent children at the sanitarium at Warm Springs, Georgia, when he himself visits there for months at a time."

As FDR's aides began to talk with Democrats around the country about the likelihood that he would run for president in 1932, they picked up more rumors on the party's grapevine. None was quite as bad as the syphilis story, but they were bad enough:

The truth, said the rumor spreaders, was that FDR had suffered from a heart attack.

Or cancer.

Or a syphilitic stroke.

Or his polio had been an act of God to punish him for terrible sins he had committed.

Then there was the old story, as a newspaper editor put it, that "a physical cripple is inclined to become an emotional and spiritual cripple."

It didn't take much of this kind of thing before FDR and his lieutenants—Howe, Ed Flynn, and Jim Farley—to realize they would have to defend against this new threat known as the "whispering campaign." They had little doubt it was being fed by powerful Democrats who hoped to block FDR from winning the nomination for president.

"I find there is a deliberate attempt to create the impression that my health is such as would make it impossible for me to fulfill the duties of President," FDR wrote a friend in 1931. "To those who know how strenuous have been the three years I have passed as Governor of this State, this is highly humorous, but it is taken with great seriousness in the southern states particularly. I shall appreciate whatever my friends may have to say in their personal correspondence to dispel this perfectly silly piece of propaganda."

The Roosevelt team decided not to ignore the rumors or try to hush them up. They would acknowledge them, then assert they simply were not true—with proof. It was not enough to point to his governorship to show he was capable of running a big executive enterprise. They had to give more evidence.

So, first, they had three prominent doctors give him a thorough medical exam, then publicized the results. The doctors declared "his organs and functions are sound in all respects . . . The chest is exceptionally well developed, and the spinal column is perfectly normal . . . and free of disease." His physical recovery from polio was likely to continue. "We believe that his powers of endurance are such as to allow him to meet all demands of private or public life."

Then they arranged for a journalist, Earle Looker, to spend enough time with FDR to write a definitive article for *Liberty*, a popular weekly magazine. The story was titled: "Is Franklin D. Roosevelt Physically Fit to Be President? A Man to Man Answer to a Nation-Wide Challenge." Looker began by saying what no other writer had said, at least not so bluntly: "It is an amazing possibility that the next President of the United States may be a cripple." For the article, three more doctors confirmed the earlier declaration—FDR was fit in every way except that "his legs are not much good to him."

The story was published in July 1931, just after FDR had sent Jim Farley on a scouting trip through the western states. If Louis Howe was Roosevelt's backroom adviser, then Farley was the perfect "outside" man. "As an Irish Catholic," one astute observer said, "he could talk on equal terms with the big-city bosses. Yet he had no Tammany links; he neither drank nor smoked; he was a man of sterling honesty and great charm; and he could also do business with perfect comfort with rural, dry, southern, and other Democratic leaders of the groups that had tended to vote Republican rather than support Al Smith in 1928." Many of the Democrats he met were enthusiastic about Roosevelt's chances and promised to vote for him at the nominating convention—but they also wanted reassurance that he was physically up to the job. Louis Howe was sending them all copies of the *Liberty* story. "I read the Liberty Magazine article today and think it is a corker," Farley wrote FDR. "I think it is a mighty fine time to have it appear because it answers fully the question that was put to me many times during the past three weeks."

———— ◆ ————

But it was not enough.

Moving into the election year of 1932, as FDR amassed more promises of support, other contenders for the Democratic nomination dropped anything from mild hints to outright bombs about his physical condition. All of them had been friends and allies of FDR in the past. But now their own interests congealed in an anyone-but-Roosevelt movement. The

Depression had become the worst economic downturn in the nation's history, and President Hoover's insensitive and stumbling responses had capsized his popularity.

The Democratic nomination for president in 1932 now looked like a first-class ticket to the White House, and every Democrat with half a national reputation wanted it.

Harry F. Byrd, the former governor of Virginia, told friends that Roosevelt was not strong enough for the presidency.

Senator William McAdoo of California, Al Smith's rival for the 1924 nomination and still hoping for the prize, said, "I can't think of Roosevelt as being equal to the demands the White House must make on its occupant in the next four years."

Frank Hague, mayor of Jersey City, New Jersey, and a close ally of Al Smith, said, "He is crippled both mentally and physically."

Then came the most painful blow.

For ten years FDR had backed Al Smith's rise to national power. FDR had submitted to Smith's plea to run for governor, and Al had attested to Roosevelt's physical fitness for the job. When Smith lost, he had declared he was through with politics, clearing the path for FDR's pursuit of the presidency.

But now the glorious chance to reverse the verdict of 1928 shimmered before Al's eyes. If FDR's campaign collapsed, Smith would be, once again, the most powerful man in the party and the most likely nominee for president.

So just before the convention, Smith told the *Saturday Evening Post* that a national campaign "requires a man of great vigor and bodily strength to stand the physical strain of it, to make no mention whatever of the tax he has to put upon his mental qualities to permit him to conduct the campaign intelligently over so long a period."

It was a savage act of sabotage. The two men, close allies for so long, would barely speak again.

In the face of all these attacks, the Roosevelt forces held strong. When the voting began at the Democratic convention in Chicago, it was touch and go for a couple of ballots. Then John Nance Garner, the powerful Speaker of the U.S. House of Representatives, instructed delegates pledged to vote for him to shift their support to FDR. Suddenly it was over. Garner was rewarded with the nomination for vice president, and FDR boarded an airplane to fly to Chicago to accept the nomination—the first nominee ever to do so in person, and the first to fly to a convention.

To the shouting delegates in Chicago Stadium he declared: "These are unprecedented and unusual times . . .

"On the farms, in the large metropolitan areas, in the smaller cities and in the villages, millions of our citizens cherish the hope that their old standards of living and of thought have not gone forever. Those millions cannot and shall not hope in vain.

"I pledge you, I pledge myself, to a new deal for the American people."

———————•◆•———————

Even the people closest to FDR—Eleanor, the children, Missy LeHand, Louis Howe—seldom saw him angry. He might snap at someone in a moment of irritation, but his steady state was so cheerful that a moment later he would be smiling again.

There were times, however, when a deep fury would rise. It tended to happen when he perceived some deliberate challenge that called his character and courage into question.

It had happened once in 1921, just before he came down with polio.

A U.S. senator named Henry Wilder Keyes, a Republican from New Hampshire, had dragged up a dusty old charge that FDR had mishandled an investigation at the Navy Department, and he laced his charges with insinuations about Roosevelt's integrity. It especially bothered FDR that Keyes was a Harvard alumnus, since FDR put great stock in the Harvard connection. He let out his feelings in a scathing letter, accusing Keyes of a "despicable action" and calling him the only Harvard man he had ever known "to be personally and willfully dishonorable . . . My only hope is that you will live long enough to appreciate that you have violated decency and truth, and that you will pray your maker for forgiveness." He thought better of sending the letter and filed it away, but he said later the incident had left him so shaken that he had been more vulnerable to the poliovirus.

It happened again in 1925, in the wake of an otherwise forgettable event at Madison Square Garden.

FDR was leading a fundraising campaign for the enormous Cathedral of Saint John the Divine, the mother church of the Episcopal diocese of New York and one of the world's largest houses of worship. So when a mass meeting was scheduled to launch the cathedral's new fund drive, naturally he was expected to attend. On the night of the meeting, FDR, with help, returned to the speaker's platform where he had performed so brilliantly a few months earlier at the Democratic National Convention. Once again, using crutches, he walked to the microphone. He introduced the Reverend William Thomas Manning, Episcopal bishop of New York, then returned to his chair and—with help—sat down.

What happened next caught the gathering by surprise. Bishop Manning said a message of support had been sent by telegram from President Calvin Coolidge, who had acceded to the White House when Warren G. Harding died of a cerebral hemorrhage two years earlier. The president's telegram had been received by Justice Edward R. Finch of New York.

The audience was invited to stand as Judge Finch read Coolidge's brief message, and they did—all except FDR, who could not stand up at a moment's notice. So he remained in his chair.

It was a trivial incident, and FDR probably would have forgotten it but for a poison-pen letter he received a day or two later. It came from a New York businessman named D. Lawson Corbett. Apparently Corbett had read a report of the meeting in the *New York Times*, which noted that "the vast audience arose and remained standing in respectful attention" for Coolidge's message.

Corbett asked FDR: "I am wondering if you, among the vast audience, rose to your feet when Justice Finch, before reading a telegram from our Beloved President, Coolidge, said: 'It gives me great pleasure to read to you the telegram which I have received from the man who more than anyone else has called us back to the faith of our fathers and reminded us that the well-being of our country, ourselves and our children must rest upon morality and religion.'"

Corbett was asking this question, he explained, because during the 1924 presidential campaign he had read a news report that said FDR had declared, "If you want to encourage crime, vote for Coolidge."

Corbett wrote: "Until that time I had always held you in very high esteem." But he believed FDR's remark about crime was so unfair that it must have turned votes to Coolidge.

It's clear that Corbett was aware of FDR's paralysis, since he finished his letter by saying, "I am happy to know that you are recovering, and hope that you will be entirely restored to health."

This time FDR put his blistering response in the mail.

He began by saying he had never made such a remark about Coolidge and crime. Then, in crystal-clear language, he let Corbett know just how vicious his question had been:

"In regard to the mass meeting in Madison Square Garden I regret to say that I was unable to rise with the rest of the audience either during the hymns or the benediction or on the occasion of the reading of the president's tele-gram; as I wear steel braces on both legs and use crutches it is impossible for me to rise or sit down without the help of two people. After presiding at the opening of the meeting and turning it over to Bishop Manning I returned to my seat, sat down and remained seated during the rest of the evening. This is, of course, not exactly pleasant for me to have to remain seated during the playing of the National Anthem and on other occasions when the audiences rise, but I am presented with the alternative of doing that or of not taking part in any community enterprises whatsoever."

It was a rare expression of his inner rage at the disease that had stolen his ability to stand up and walk on his own, and at anyone who failed to see he was no less a man than he had ever been.

That deep anger rose once more in the spring of 1932, in the midst of Roosevelt's race for the presidential nomination, and this time it was more consequential.

FDR and Herbert Hoover had been casually friendly back in World War I, when both were based in Washington. FDR had even suggested that Hoover, who had not yet declared himself a Republican, might one day run for president. Lately, watching his old acquaintance in the White House, FDR thought him a failure as a leader, but he bore the president no ill will—not until the evening when Hoover hosted a dinner for the nation's governors and their wives at the White House.

FDR and Eleanor arrived a little early, knowing they would have to walk slowly into position as the governors lined up to stand and greet the Hoovers. They reached their place in line, Eleanor remembered, "and then we stood and waited. Twenty minutes passed and the president and Mrs. Hoover did not appear. Every kind of rumor flew about the room. It was said we were waiting for some of the governors, two of whom never appeared. My husband was twice offered a chair, but he evidently thought that if he showed any weakness someone might make an adverse political story out of it, so he refused each time. It seemed as though he were being deliberately put through an endurance test, but he stood the whole evening very well, though the one-half hour before President and Mrs. Hoover appeared was an ordeal. This idea may seem preposterous but in political life you grow suspicious."

In situations, certainly, and in others when he was not simply angry but resolute, Roosevelt would say "my Dutch is up," a proud reference to the stubborn Netherlanders of his family tree. Now, with the national campaign about to start, he was about to say it again.

—————◆—————

He was the nominee of his party. But he was beginning the national campaign in the shadow of a doubt.

Powerful Democrats were beginning to hope for a landslide victory. Why should Roosevelt take a chance on a full-tilt campaign that might leave him exhausted? He could stay in New York, give a few national speeches on the radio, and win walking away. Many in the party's upper tiers thought he should cancel the plans for a big western campaign trip, and they sent Jim Farley to Albany to deliver that message to the governor.

"Big Jim" and Roosevelt were both well aware the whispering campaign was still thriving out in the country. They knew that when FDR had visited Warm Springs a few weeks earlier, rumormongers had spread tales that he had been carried to his quarters on a stretcher and that he had stayed there in seclusion to be treated for a mysterious illness. They knew all about what one reporter called "the cleverly managed propaganda which depicted Mr. Roosevelt as a weak man." They may well have heard that Herbert Hoover and his aides were saying, behind closed doors in the White House, that Roosevelt would be the best possible Democratic nominee if only the public could see his "helplessness."

When New York Republicans had talked like that in 1928, FDR had taken a fierce pride in showing voters how much physical stamina he really had. The whispers about his health had gone on ever since. Even many of his true friends and allies couldn't quite believe he had the strength for a national campaign. He had stood and stood on aching legs while President Hoover made him wait. He had listened to friends urge him to take it easy, save his energy, and coast to the finish line.

FDR asked Farley, "Jim, what do you think yourself?"

"I think you ought to go," Farley said, breaking into a grin. "And I know you are going anyway."

"That's right," Roosevelt said. "My Dutch is up."

———— • ◆ • ————

In mid-September a six-car train called the Roosevelt Special crossed the Mississippi River at St. Louis just as news was coming in that Maine, a rock-solid Republican state, had elected a Democrat as governor—a good omen for FDR's national campaign.

In the crowds that came out to see the Democratic nominee for president, many people were in the grip of a quiet desperation.

Since 1930, month by month, things had gone steadily from bad to worse to disastrous. The value of companies had been rising all through the prosperous 1920s. People had thought the American economy might never stop growing. Now solid companies large and small were going under. In the great industrial cities, factories closed one assembly line, then another, leaving millions of workers unable to buy food or pay rent. Mines closed. Stores closed. The tonnage of goods hauled over the nation's railroads dropped and dropped and dropped. As the wages of people in the cities fell, farmers in the countryside had to cut the prices they charged for their grain, milk, meat, and eggs—down and down and down—and by 1932, many farmers were so desperate there was talk of revolution. People hanging on to their jobs lived in fear of the next round of closings. Dozens of banks shut their doors, then hundreds. The entire banking system teetered on the edge of a general collapse.

President Hoover's halting half measures had failed. When destitute veterans of World War I gathered in Washington to ask for early payment of the bonuses they'd earned for their war service, Hoover sent armed soldiers to drive them away. The Roosevelts were appalled when they read about it. FDR wondered how he had ever thought Hoover could be a good president.

He'd concluded "there is nothing inside the man but jelly." He thought of the veterans pushed out of the capital, bringing nothing home to their families. "They're probably camping on the roads leading out of Washington," he said. "They must be in terrible shape." In and around cities and towns, families who had lost their homes hammered up shacks with scrap lumber and sheet metal. They called these makeshift settlements Hoovervilles.

———————— ◆ ————————

In big cities FDR delivered speeches to convention-sized crowds. He spoke about the farm crisis to twelve thousand in Topeka, Kansas. He spoke about the railroad crisis to ten thousand at the great Mormon Tabernacle in Salt Lake City. He spoke about the crisis in international trade to sixteen thousand at the Civic Auditorium in Seattle. He spoke on harnessing rivers for electrical power in a packed arena in Portland.

These were huge audiences. But he could have stayed home and given the same speeches by radio to audiences numbering in the millions. The point of the trip had more to do with the stops he made in small towns along his route. As he said to a thousand people who came to see him at the railroad station in Goodland, Kansas (population: 3,626), "We are going through the country doing a very simple thing: We are showing ourselves to you."

What did that mean? Simply what it said—he was showing people that, contrary to what they might have heard, he had all the strength and stamina needed for a demanding cross-country journey with speeches and meetings all along the way. If he could do that, could anyone say he wasn't strong enough to be president?

During his first campaign for governor, in 1928, he had spoken often about his comeback from polio. Not in 1932. He never mentioned it. He let his performance make the case. He expected the reporters on the campaign train to make the point to their readers, and they did.

"The governor appears in the best of trim," remarked a reporter for the

Chicago Tribune, "in high spirits and having lost none of the vigorous delivery which marks all his speeches."

He was showing "that he is not a wheelchair invalid incapable of meeting the physical ordeals of the Presidential Office," wrote a reporter for the *Los Angeles Times*, and indeed, "the governor gives the impression of a man in excellent physical condition, capable of meeting as strenuous campaigning as anyone else."

———— ◆ ————

As the people watched FDR, he was watching them. Shortly after the trip, at the townhouse in New York, he chatted with a small circle of family and associates over dinner. He was thinking about the faces he had seen in the West.

"They are the faces of people in want," he said. "I don't mean the unemployed alone. Of course, they would take anything. I mean those who still have jobs and don't know how long they'll last. They have the frightened look of lost children. And I don't mean physical want alone. There is something more . . . a kind of yearning—'We're caught in something we don't understand; perhaps this fellow can help us out.'"

———— ◆ ————

He won, of course, and in the terrible winter that followed, he prepared to assume the presidency.

He had been courageous, but as with anyone, his courage was not the absence of fear. On the night before his inauguration at the U.S. Capitol on March 4, 1933, he told his son Jimmy that he needed Jimmy's prayers, since he wasn't sure he was strong enough for the job.

Then, the next day, under lowering clouds at the U.S. Capitol, before one hundred thousand spectators, he walked to the rostrum, took the constitutional oath of office, and said, "The only thing we have to fear is fear itself."

On May 2, 1997, a national memorial to Franklin Roosevelt was unveiled on the Mall in Washington, D.C. It covered seven and a half acres not far from the memorials to Washington, Jefferson, and Lincoln.

The visitors saw not a towering obelisk, like Washington's, or a temple, like Jefferson's and Lincoln's. It was a granite park that led them through a series of tableaux in which running water was the central element, from a stream to a roaring waterfall. There were statues of ordinary people waiting in a Great Depression breadline. There was a statue of Eleanor Roosevelt, in tribute to the world-sized role she played as First Lady of the United States, political activist, and advocate for peace.

And there was, of course, a statue of FDR. The figure was seated with a cape swirled around his legs and chair, gazing with a hero's vision at the far horizon.

There was a lot of arguing about that statue.

Unlike in FDR's own time, the disabled people of the United States—who in the 1990s numbered nearly fifty million—had found their voices and organized to claim their rights, many of which had been guaranteed by federal law in the Americans with Disabilities Act of 1990. They were certainly not of a single mind about the statue of FDR. But many of them believed it was wrong to shroud the truth—that he had depended on crutches, braces, and a wheelchair—under a flowing cape.

An advocate for disability rights named Yvonne Duffy, who had been struck by polio when she was two years old, spoke for many when she wrote: "I remember my mother telling me, straightening her back proudly as she spoke, that polio had never stopped Franklin Roosevelt from becoming president. Her message was clear: Even a child with a disability like mine could aspire to be president . . . Times have changed in the 50 years since FDR's death . . . No longer is a physical impairment viewed as something shameful, something to be hidden. But you wouldn't know this from the actions of the Franklin Delano Roosevelt Memorial Commission . . . They would make my mother's inspirational story to a disabled child a pathetic lie."

Duffy and many others demanded a change. Roosevelt must be depicted as an obviously disabled man, they said.

On the other side of the argument were people thinking about what FDR himself would have wanted. David B. Roosevelt, one of Elliott's children, said those who argued for a visible wheelchair were trying to rewrite history. "My grandfather guarded his condition closely," Roosevelt wrote. "FDR was most certainly not shamed by his condition. He realized, however, that the difficult decisions he made surrounding the Great Depression, World War II and other events of the times required a vigorous leader who inspired faith in the people he served. Unfortunately, during the 1930s and '40s this nation was not as enlightened concerning people with disabilities as it is today." (Not all Roosevelts agreed. Anne Roosevelt, a daughter of John's, remarked, "We should portray him as he was, and as he was, he wore braces.")

The advocates' reply to David Roosevelt was that FDR, had he lived in the 1990s, would have embraced the modern disabilities movement and endorsed the inclusion of a wheelchair in his memorial. (Not many remembered that when Roosevelt, as president, was asked about any future monument to his memory, he said he would like there to be a simple stone block the size of his desk, engraved with his name and installed by the National Archives Building on Pennsylvania Avenue. His wish was granted in 1965.)

In the end, the disability advocates got their way—mostly. The original statue of FDR in the concealing cape remained. But in 2001 a second statue was added to the memorial, this one showing him in glasses and his favorite slouch hat, casually seated in his simple wheelchair.

———————— ◆ ————————

These heated discussions had to do with *how* FDR was portrayed. They tended to overlook the larger matter of *why* he had been portrayed in a national memorial in the first place, and on a scale that placed him at the level of Washington, Jefferson, and Lincoln in the nation's memory.

The memorial was built because Roosevelt was beyond a doubt the most influential president of his century.

In the early months of his first term in office, known ever after simply as the "Hundred Days," he won Congress's agreement to a blizzard of innovative programs designed to heal the worst ills of the Great Depression—emergency measures to put the jobless to work, to save the banking system from collapse, to restore businesses and farms to productivity. In the first of his great environmental programs, he brought thousands of young men into a Civilian Conservation Corps and put them to work planting trees and fighting forest fires. In one of the hardest-hit regions of the country, he established the sprawling Tennessee Valley Authority, a regional plan to generate badly needed electric power while preventing disastrous floods and soil erosion.

The country gasped at the audacity of his program, then largely embraced it. Roosevelt was a tonic for sick souls.

More enormous reforms followed in the wake of the Hundred Days, both before and after FDR's reelection in a landslide in 1936. There were programs to help young people get jobs and go to college, to provide Social Security pensions to old people, to help workers organize in labor unions. In a gigantic construction campaign to give jobs to the unemployed and stimulate the economy, his administration built dams, bridges, and tunnels; civic auditoriums and schools; highways and post offices and airports. There was even a program to put unemployed artists, writers, and musicians to work, practicing their crafts in the public interest.

All these laws, programs, and projects became known by the term FDR had introduced in the 1932 campaign—the New Deal. He wasn't talking about a business deal. He was talking about quitting an old game, shuffling the cards, and starting over.

Month by month, year by year, the country began to climb out of the crisis. It was slow. High unemployment continued; people were still hungry. Critics on the left said FDR's activist program wasn't enough, that more radical measures were needed. On the right, conservatives began to call him a "traitor to his class" and warned of a slide into socialism. But even they had to concede that his strong show of action may have headed off a revolution.

In 1937 the rising economy took another downward lurch. The president's critics called it the "Roosevelt recession." But by 1940, the nation, though still scared and certainly scarred, was looking backward at the Great Depression. That was due in part to the New Deal. But it was also due to a new crisis, this one across the oceans. American factories were roaring again, making materials for war.

By the precedent set by George Washington but never written into law, presidents left office after two terms. Roosevelt's two terms were nearly up.

But in the spring of 1940, the Nazi armies of Adolf Hitler swept across western Europe and threatened to invade Great Britain. The military leaders of Japan had conquered much of China and were demanding concessions from the United States and its allies in the western Pacific Ocean. Roosevelt was deeply wary of the threats these dictators posed to U.S. interests. But he had played his cards cautiously, knowing most Americans wanted to stay out of war.

With the Nazi armies' *blitzkrieg* drive to the English Channel, the crisis seemed so grave that many Americans could not imagine proceeding without Franklin Roosevelt in the White House. He agreed to run for a third term, the only president to do so, and he won.

So he was in office on December 7, 1941, when the Japanese attacked the U.S. naval fleet at Pearl Harbor, Hawaii. The next day, Germany, Japan's ally, declared war on the United States as well.

Roosevelt said that "Doctor New Deal" must now become "Doctor Win-the-War."

His most consequential decision as commander-in-chief was to declare Germany the primary enemy, despite the thirst for revenge that so many Americans felt in response to the Japanese "sneak attack." Historians have judged the "Atlantic First" strategy to be the right call. If Germany had been allowed to conquer its remaining foes in Europe—the United Kingdom and the Soviet Union—then Hitler would have stood astride half the world. So Roosevelt directed the navy to hold off the Japanese threat while the United States armed the British and the Soviets, all the while building up armies and weapons for a great strike back at Germany. That came when Allied forces attacked the German occupiers of France on June 6, 1944, known as D-Day.

In both theaters of war, despite horrific losses, the United States and its allies made slow but steady progress against their enemies. By the fall of 1944, when Roosevelt was elected to a fourth term as president, there was little doubt about the eventual result. It was just a question of how long the war would last and how great the suffering would be.

Through those twelve dark years of pain and upheaval, Roosevelt's leadership was the beacon in the darkness. Because he so evidently believed that all would be well in the end, people took hope. And it was no small thing that they knew he had come through a great personal ordeal, rising from near death to reclaim his life and his future. In the end, nobody much cared whether he could walk.

———————◆◆———————

On April 12, 1945, in his white cottage at Warm Springs, he put his hand to head and said, "I have a terrific headache." A blood vessel had burst in his brain. A few minutes later he was dead. He had been in poor health from high blood pressure and a bad heart for many months. Probably he should not have run for his fourth term. But he had beaten one disease. Perhaps he thought he could beat another as he had the first—by trying this and trying that, coming back again and again, keeping everlastingly at it until death itself might give up in the face of his smiling persistence.

One time he had tossed off an idea for some big project to an aide.

The man said, "Mr. President, you can't do that."

FDR replied, "I've done a lot of things I can't do."

———————◆◆———————

The way Roosevelt portrayed his disability in the intense spotlight of the presidency has been called a "splendid deception." That isn't quite right.

Disability itself is the deception. It makes able-bodied people misunderstand how capable the disabled person actually is.

Of course there were things Roosevelt could not do. Those things did not include serving as president of the United States. He suffered more from the *appearance* of disability than from disability itself. Appearances, it is often said, are deceiving.

As president, FDR acted the part of the extraordinarily capable man he was. He knew the value of a great performance. Once, in a meeting with the movie actor and director Orson Welles, he is said to have remarked, "You know, Orson, there are two great actors in America. You are the *other* one."

Certainly there was no conspiratorial cover-up, as many people believe. Anyone paying attention to public affairs knew the president had made a comeback from an attack of infantile paralysis. The fact was trumpeted every year on his birthday, when fundraising events called the President's Birthday Balls raised money for the National Foundation for Infantile Paralysis, an organization FDR had started at Warm Springs, as he was proud to say. (The foundation would change its name to the March of Dimes. It paid for most of the research that led to vaccines that would virtually eradicate polio around the world.) So his polio was hardly a secret.

It's true that he did what he could to dampen public awareness of just how handicapped he was. His press aides discouraged reporters from referring to it—though they occasionally did—and asked photographers not to take his picture in physically awkward moments, a request they almost always granted. He never used his wheelchair in public. Since there was no television news, FDR's movements were not constantly in the public eye, as they would be today. So the average person wound up thinking the president was simply lame.

Of course, his condition was worse than lameness. He never gained any greater ability to walk than he achieved with his physical therapists at Warm Springs in 1928.

He kept that fact on the down-low for the same old reasons. He didn't want pity. He didn't want to fall in public. (He did so as president at least once, during the 1936 campaign, though it attracted little attention.) He didn't want people to feel uncomfortable in his presence. And undoubtedly he saw no reason to hand ammunition to his political enemies. He had learned they would use any evidence of his paralysis to their own advantage.

In the privacy of the White House he had himself pushed around in a wheelchair, by far his preferred means of mobility. For meetings and receptions he followed the same routines he had established as governor in Albany. He preferred to have his personal helpers or the Secret Service get him in position with as few people seeing his movements as possible. If there was no other way—at his inaugurations, for instance, with many thousands watching—he put on his damnable braces and walked.

If he had to be carried where people could see, he dispelled the awkwardness with a quick remark and a smile. After the death in 1938 of an old friend, Dr. Cary Grayson, Woodrow Wilson's personal physician, FDR paid a private visit to Grayson's widow at her home in Washington. When his car pulled up in front, Grayson's sons came out to greet him. There was a sidewalk twenty yards long from the curb to the porch. The Graysons watched as two Secret Service agents opened the rear door. Then, one of the sons recalled, "they cradled the president between them, his strong arms and hands over their shoulders and his legs lifelessly dangling from their firmly locked hands. With a jaunty smile, he said to my brothers and me, 'Boys, you'll have to excuse me, but it's a relief not to have to wear pounds of steel on my legs today.'"

People who saw him helped into or out of an automobile or a train car were startled. It was the same when people watched him up close as he did his walking-with-braces performance. Afterward they would say they'd never known how bad off he was. Yet as FDR surely realized, he never paid a political price for these small revelations. If anything, people came away more impressed than they had been before.

The great newspaper columnist Ernie Pyle, who would go on to fame as an overseas correspondent in World War II, noticed this effect once during the 1936 campaign.

Pyle happened to be in Rapid City, South Dakota, when Roosevelt's entourage came to town. They had rooms in the same hotel. On a Sunday morning, Pyle watched from his window as the president returned from church. A crowd was on the sidewalk, waiting to see him. Pyle wrote about the moment from memory a few weeks later:

"Now there have been, out of what I have always felt to be a fine sense of consideration, few mentions in print or in picture of the president's partial paralysis. But it seems to me there can be no violation of good taste in relating anything as beautiful as what happened at Rapid City that day.

"The crowd stopped clapping, and stood silently watching, as the car stopped at the hotel entrance. It was a 7-passenger touring car, with the top down. The president's two sons and his daughter-in-law got out ahead of him.

"Then, while everybody waited, the president . . . with his powerful arms slid himself forward onto the spare seat. Then he turned a little and put his legs out the door and over the running board, with his feet almost to the curb. Gus Gennerich, the president's bodyguard and personal assistant, stood ready to help. But he was not needed. You could almost have heard a pin drop. The president put both hands on one leg and pushed downward, locking the jointed steel brace at his knee. He slowly did the same with the other leg.

"Then he put his hands on the side of the car, and with his arms lifted his body out and up and onto his legs. He straightened up. I have never seen a man so straight.

"And at that moment the tenseness broke, and the crowd applauded. The president's back was to the crowd, and he did not look around. It was brief and restrained applause.

"I don't know, but I doubt that that has ever happened to the president before. It was the tenderest, most admiring tribute to courage I have ever seen. It was such a poignant thing, so surprising, so spontaneous. It was as though they were saying with their hands, 'We know we shouldn't, but we've got to.'

"When I turned from the window there was a lump in my throat, and there would have been in yours, too."

A NOTE ON SOURCES

This story draws on many of the same sources I used when writing *The Man He Became: How FDR Defied Polio to Win the Presidency* (2013). But this is a wholly new book, written for younger readers.

By far the most important sources for understanding Franklin Roosevelt's experience of polio are what historians call original sources—the letters, memos, diaries, and other writings that come directly from those who took part in these events or observed them from up close. Most of the original sources I used are housed in the Franklin D. Roosevelt Presidential Library in Hyde Park, New York. They are kept in many different collections that make up the papers of the Roosevelt family—FDR's personal and official papers, Eleanor Roosevelt's papers, a set of family papers donated by the Roosevelts' children, Louis Howe's papers, and many more. There is one slim folder titled "Infantile Paralysis," but the great majority of references to polio are scattered in myriad other folders. Finding them, I like to say, was like looking for a hundred needles in a thousand haystacks, but the search was always fun. The FDR Library also contains a comprehensive collection of Roosevelt's speeches, all of them available online. The library's enormous collection of photographs is another important source of information—showing, to take one small example, that FDR as governor of New York often allowed himself to be photographed with his braces showing at the ankles, which tends to deflate the notion of a conspiratorial cover-up of his condition.

Another important source was newspapers, especially for the campaigns in 1928 and 1932. Some major papers, like the *New York Times* and the *Washington Post*, make their old editions available online. A great many other stories would be very hard to find were it not for the voluminous scrapbooks of press clippings that FDR's staff maintained. These, too, are at the FDR Library.

Books by members of FDR's family and close associates were invaluable. The most important for telling the polio story were Frances Perkins, *The Roosevelt I Knew* (1946); Samuel Rosenman, *Working With Roosevelt* (1952); Eleanor Roosevelt's two memoirs, *This Is My Story* (1939) and *This I Remember* (1949); and James Farley, *Behind the Ballots* (1938). James and Elliott Roosevelt both wrote two books about their parents. Elliott's, especially, raise doubts about the reliability of a grown child remembering early years with parents. In 1949, Anna Roosevelt Halsted published a valuable series of magazine articles titled "My Life With FDR" in a magazine she helped to create, *The Woman*. It's a shame Anna never wrote a full memoir, as she seems to have known her father the best of all the children. Two memoirs by Anna's son, Curtis Roosevelt, *Too Close to the Sun* (2008) and *Upstairs at the Roosevelts'* (2017), give fascinating glimpses of the family's private life. As a teenager, Curtis lived with his mother and grandparents in the White House for much of World War II, and his account of FDR's dealings with disability are detailed and insightful. (I gained a great deal from a long interview with Mr. Roosevelt, whose voice sounded astonishingly like FDR's. He died in 2016.)

Several books by contemporary reporters fill in important details, including John Gunther, *Roosevelt in Retrospect: A Profile in History* (1950), which remains one of the best sources on FDR's many-faceted life; Ernest Lindley, *Franklin D. Roosevelt: A Career in Progressive Democracy* (rev. ed., 1934)—Lindley covered FDR's early campaigns and knew him well; and Earle Looker, *This Man Roosevelt* (1932). Looker was the writer hired by the Roosevelt campaign to write a magazine story about FDR's health. That casts a shadow on his reliability, but the book is an important document of the campaign, at least.

Many general biographies of FDR have been published, of course, but most move quickly through the polio story. The exception is Geoffrey C. Ward's two-volume biography, which takes FDR from his birth to 1928, with a great deal of information about his parents and ancestors—*Before the Trumpet: Young Franklin Roosevelt, 1882–1905* (1985) and *A First-Class Temperament: The Emergence of Franklin Roosevelt, 1905–1928* (1989). Ward's account is deep and rich, and his coverage of FDR's struggle with polio is based in part on his interviews with people who worked with FDR at Warm Springs. Other biographies I relied on included James MacGregor Burns's two volumes, especially *Roosevelt: The Lion and the Fox* (1956); Frank Freidel, *Franklin D. Roosevelt: The Ordeal* (1954), the second volume of Freidel's five; Rexford G. Tugwell, *The Democratic Roosevelt* (1957); and Joseph P. Lash, *Eleanor and Franklin* (1971). I used the excellent biographies of FDR's closest aides during the period covered: Alfred B. Rollins, *Roosevelt and Howe* (1962); and Kathryn Smith, *The Gatekeeper: Missy LeHand, FDR, and the Untold Story of the Partnership That Defined a Presidency* (2016).

Readers will gain a deeper understanding of FDR's life in the context of Hyde Park from F. Kennon Moody's excellent account, *FDR and His Hudson Valley Neighbors* (2013).

Besides *The Man He Became*, there are five other books, all of them useful, about Roosevelt's experience with polio. They are: Turnley Walker, *Roosevelt and the Warm Springs Story* (1953); Jean Gould, *A Good Fight* (1960); Theo Lippmann Jr., *The Squire of Warm Springs: FDR in Georgia, 1924–1945* (1977); Richard Thayer Goldberg, *The Making of Franklin D. Roosevelt: Triumph Over Disability* (1981); and Hugh Gregory Gallagher, *FDR's Splendid Deception* (1985). Another good source for the Warm Springs story, with many photographs, is Kaye Lanning Minchew, *A President in Our Midst: Franklin Delano Roosevelt in Georgia* (2016).

Overviews of all aspects of FDR's life appear in Otis L. Graham Jr. and Meghan Robinson Wander, eds., *Franklin D. Roosevelt, His Life and Times: An Encyclopedic View* (1985).

The reader knows how much I relied on the observations of the Roosevelts' friend Frances Perkins, who knew FDR well from the beginning of his career in politics and served as secretary of the U.S. Department of Labor throughout his terms as president. She recounts her memories and her ideas about FDR not only in *The Roosevelt I Knew* but also in the interviews she gave to the Columbia University Center for Oral History Research. These deeply detailed and fascinating interviews, which cover Perkins's entire life and career, can be heard online in their entirety at the center's website.

ACKNOWLEDGMENTS

· ·

Teaching the craft of telling true stories has forced me to think harder about how stories work. Talking about the craft with students as they try it themselves is a pleasure. So I'm grateful to my students at Miami University for our work together.

Two of those students, now on their way to illustrious careers, lent time and talent to this project. Megan Zahneis provided important research on the 1932 campaign and on the debate over the Roosevelt Memorial. She also shared her reflections on the experience of disability, which have influenced my interpretation of FDR at numerous points. Samantha Brunn gave critical aid with photographs.

No historian can write a page without archivists and librarians, who keep the materials of history alive, organized, and within reach. For this book I'm especially grateful to the archival staff of the Franklin D. Roosevelt Presidential Library and Museum. Thanks, too, to Matthew Schaefer of the Herbert Hoover Presidential Library and Museum.

At Henry Holt and Company, Christy Ottaviano and her colleagues were superb. I'm especially indebted to Christy for her faith in the project, her excellent judgment, and her patience. Thanks, too, to Taylor Pitts and Barbara Bakowski for their thorough and astute copyediting.

At Fletcher & Company, Melissa Chinchillo represented the book with her usual skill and good cheer.

I'm grateful to John U. Bacon, who helped me get it over the finish line.

I'm lucky to belong to a big extended family of book lovers. Thanks to all the Tobins, Kellers, Wilsons, and LaFaves for keeping the torch alive and the business afloat.

But Leesa Erickson Tobin deserves by far the most thanks, for absolutely everything.

INDEX

•••••••••••••••••••••••••••